AUTHOR OF
PROMOTION

Discovering God's Promotional Plan for You

DAVE KING

CONTENTS

Foreword

Last spring I was driving to a speaking engagement and working through various introductory openings but coming up empty. I was the keynote speaker at a leadership symposium at a four-year college. After parking my car, I walked slowly up to the main campus auditorium with my daughter Cassia, looked over to her, and said, "I got nothin'." I resigned myself to delivering a clumsy opening. If you are an experienced speaker, you know the feeling of coming up empty with your introduction and the terror associated with being handed a microphone and having nothing relevant to open with. No jokes, no clever one-liners . . . nothin'.

The auditorium was filling up as I walked in. The president of the sorority, whom I will call "Mary," came up to me and introduced herself. Mary is the one who had invited me to speak at this annual fraternity/sorority leadership symposium and mental health awareness meeting. We had first spoken weeks prior to the event while she was in the hospital behavioral science unit. Throughout her teenage years, Mary had struggled with depression, anxiety, and suicidal thoughts and had now experienced a relapse.

When it was time to begin the meeting, Mary stepped up to the microphone to welcome everyone and to introduce me. She began by telling her peers about her own struggles with depression and anxiety. Tears flowed freely as she painfully recanted some of her darkest hours. Tears turned to sobs as she was overwhelmed with emotion. This wonderful and powerful daughter looked to me for help. "I can't go on," Mary told me softly. "Can you introduce yourself?" As she bravely gathered herself, she went over and sat quietly in the front row.

Grasping the handheld microphone off the podium stand, I walked up to the front row of the auditorium and peered at the room full of young college students absorbing the emotional beginning. Wiping tears from my eyes, I began by saying, "Hi. I'm Dave King, executive director of the iMatter Foundation. But tonight I'm a dad."

I praised Mary for her courage and inner strength, and for the next forty-five minutes I honored, loved on, and encouraged the brilliant young minds and hearts of the students who were in that room. Each person was looking for affirmation and someone to tell him or her, "Everything is going to be okay." As the evening progressed, I met and loved on dozens of young adults who had suffered the effects of suicidal thoughts and tendencies.

This book is dedicated to Mary and the tens of thousands of kids I have had the honor of serving in a twenty-seven-year coaching career and as executive director of the iMatter Foundation. You are amazing sons and daughters. I love you all.

"For the earnest expectation of the creation eagerly waits for the revealing of the sons of God."[1]

---

1 Romans 8:19

Preface

I have known Dave since he was eighteen when I had the privilege of leading him to the Lord at a venue where my band was playing in upstate New York. We have been friends for the last thirty-six years–running hard for the kingdom—sometimes intentionally and other times unknowingly. Little did we know that the Father was grooming us for this current season of our lives. Through our exposure to various marketplaces, we have discovered a lack of leaders due to the absence of fathers.

Author of Promotion is a response to these findings. God the Father is ultimately the One who promotes us. He is the Author and the Finisher of our journeys. His desire is for sons and daughters to be revealed to all of creation and bring about heaven's impact. Dave's book has keys that will allow its readers to connect concepts, feelings, and thoughts perhaps considered but often misunderstood. The concepts of this book have the capacity to invite heaven's answers to respond to this much needed challenge of becoming leaders who represent God's heart appropriately. My hope is that this book will stir your thinking and allow you to consider the eternal answers now being made available for men and women who want to impact our world.

SCOTT LOWMASTER
SENIOR PASTOR OF THE JOURNEY CENTER
FOUNDER OF THE iMATTER FOUNDATION

Section 1

~

AUTHOR AND OWNER OF PROMOTION

Chapter 1

God-ordained Leadership

I sat in stunned silence in part waiting to see if there was more coming, but mostly in a kind of holy reverence with a side of unworthiness after a direct encounter with the Most High God. As I overlooked the Chesapeake Bay on the Eastern Shore of Maryland, I remained frozen in place, head still, jaw dropped, trying to process what had just happened.

My week had started typically enough. I was on a work-related road trip, intensely missing my wife and two daughters. However, it was on these road trips I learned the value of being alone with the Godhead. I would wake up alone, work alone, dine alone, and return to the hotel to sleep alone. These were extended times of solitude focused on God doing the talking. Similar to a kid's staring contest, this was a "no talking" contest, a game of "Whoever speaks first loses." If God is not talking, neither am I. I like it best when I win.

The trip started with personal worship, highlighted when I pulled over on the Pennsylvania Turnpike. Our exchange of love had so spilled over that through my tears of love and joy, I could no longer safely drive along the crowded highway. After I recovered, I finished driving to the Eastern Shore and ended the day early.

The next day started with something in the air. I could feel the Holy Spirit calling to my spirit man, "Son, posture yourself." I began work but kept my ear bent toward heaven. Now I sat overlooking the Chesapeake Bay eating a sandwich. It was as quiet as it had been all morning, and God broke the silence with one of those millisecond downloads of understanding.

He spoke: "Son, here is what I am tasking you with." These words were followed by glimpses of promotion and leadership. I saw a leadership structure unlike anything else I had ever considered. Instead of corporate *church*, this was corporate *heaven*. I saw vision, mantle, and glory as the Holy Spirit revealed a promotion only He could author, a promotion depending on only two provisions: God's faithfulness and our raw obedience. As His faithfulness is absolute, I knew my raw obedience was the only thing in question.

Under the weight of the mantle being presented by the Author of promotion, I crumbled and weakly answered, "Father, I can't do this. I'm not strong enough," but I continued. Quoting Jesus, I mumbled, "Nevertheless not my will, but Yours, be done."[1]

That day was in the spring of 2008, and since that time my life has drastically been altered. I retired from twenty-seven years of coaching college and high school basketball and football to partner with Scott Lowmaster, the visionary and founder of the iMatter Foundation. I left my senior vice president position at a large timberland marketing and management firm to build the King Timberlands Consulting Group (KTCG), and my wife and I moved to Elmira, New York, to help build and lead a growing movement within the Journey Center church pastored by Scott.

---

1 Luke 22:42, adapted

God's favor followed His promotion. In our first three years, KTCG successfully marketed over $100 million in timberland assets. I also pioneered an entrepreneurs' club that is developing and launching new businesses and leaders. We have helped launch businesses in Alabama, Pennsylvania, and New York. These businesses are founded on kingdom principles by sons and daughters of our Most High God, partnered with their Lord, Savior, and intimate friend, Jesus, empowered by the Holy Spirit and anointed into their promotion authored by I AM: the Author and Owner of our promotion.

God Ordains Our Promotion

Jesus's earthly ministry promoted others. His ministry started and ended with promotion. His arrival was announced by leveling the playing field with kings and shepherds. Never exclusive, His was a ministry for the inclusive. Jesus promoted the poor in spirit, the persecuted, and the meek. He promoted the multitudes to be the salt of the earth, a city on a hill, and the light of the world. Positions religion says are reserved for the most pious.

Jesus promoted a tax collector, rough-and-tough fishermen, a thief, a zealot, elitist brothers, and women. He transferred his jurisdictional authority to the twelve, then to the seventy, then to the multitudes.[2] Jesus promoted a Samaritan woman caught in a lifestyle of infidelity to influence a village unto salvation. He promoted children and widows and orphans and prostitutes and Romans.

Jesus disregarded cultural biases against women by meeting with one of them in the heat of the day alone at Jacob's well. He freed them from unholy ritualistic blame for acts of sexual sin,[3] and He allowed

---

2 Luke 9:49–50

3 John 8:7

them into His inner circle and gave them the first glimpse of His resurrection.

Jesus challenged the rich to be poor[4] and claimed the poor to be rich.[5] Jesus dispensed with racial bias.[6] He took a wrecking ball to elitism by choosing the lowly and socially disqualified to build His kingdom upon.

Jesus provided an early example of the heart of the heavenly Father. His actions were perfectly congruent with the Father's design. He did only what the Father did and said what the Father said.[7] Jesus's example is our example.

> Jesus took a wrecking ball to elitism by choosing the lowly and socially disqualified to build His kingdom upon.

In the Godhead's eyes, we are all born into leadership. We hold the grandest title available on earth. We are sons and daughters of the Most High God, full-blood brothers and sisters of the Firstborn. We are empowered and anointed by the Holy Spirit.

A Collision Between Belief and Behavior

It is difficult and nearly impossible to instill into every child, young and old, the concept that he or she was born into leadership.[8] For most people, a life of demotion and lack of acknowledgment from others begins at an early age. When our belief systems are developed from life

---

4 Matthew 19:21

5 Mark 12:41

6 Luke 10:33

7 John 5:19

8 Matthew 19:26

experience instead of biblical truth, we are on a collision course with that unhealthy belief system.

For many of us, life experience comes from the influence of a worldly culture heavy laden with attempts to disqualify us from God's promotion. Our culture disqualifies sons and daughters because of race, religion, gender, lifestyle, body type, social status, economic class, and more. We are told what we cannot do and what we do not qualify for. Because of these disqualifiers, we learn we will never qualify. This separation places people into classes and is the basis of class warfare. Instead of living in abundance as sons and daughters of the King, class warfare promotes an orphan status positioned in lack.

Jesus confronted class warfare from the onset of His ministry and kept the pressure on it right through His last recorded statements. He uncovered how the world system had crept into the church. In the world corporate structure, leadership positions come with all kinds of titles. Leaders know they have been promoted when they gain a title, but with these titles the minority rule the majority. The majority are considered the workforce, people who are relegated to simply accomplishing what their supervisors tell them to do.

In the world corporate structure, higher-level positions are restricted by limitations in size of the organization, cost in terms of salary and benefit packages, and the availability of such positions. Leaders are selected from pools of the best-educated candidates or candidates with the appropriate breeding or connections. This leadership prototype is based on a production mind-set that has few leaders in charge. The remaining employees use their individual gifts to accomplish a narrow set of goals and objectives. This task-oriented production mind-set minimizes the importance of relationship and restrains promotion.

Corporate Structure Invades the Church

Unlike the limits of the world corporate structure, the kingdom of heaven has a large and far-reaching vision. There is no beginning and no end. There is no limit to size or growth potential. There are no limits on leadership positions. The only limits to promotion are what God places on us and what we place on ourselves.

In truth, God's heart is not only that we attain the highest position available in His organization, but He also assures us that promotion is not something we need to work or ask for. We have been grafted into the position; we just need to be obedient. Why, then, does the Western church frequently resemble corporate America with its leadership structure? As sad as it is, a combination of spiritual elitism and prodigal heirs has created a perfect storm that can invade our churches.

The concept that the people relegated to the base workforce are actually promoted to senior leadership in the kingdom was the very principle that alienated Jesus from the church hierarchy. At the outset, He seemed at odds with every church title of the day: "Pharisees," "Sadducees," "elders," and "teachers of the Law." All individuals with such titles appeared united in their opposition to Him. The church leaders believed Jesus was stripping them of their power base, and this was the primary reason for their adversity to Him. Jesus empowered His followers in corresponding teachings in Matthew 10, Mark 6, Luke 9, and Luke 10 and then released them into His kingdom ministry. Jesus transferred His authority first to the twelve, then to the seventy as a prophetic act of what was to come. This threatened to topple the church government that denied status and equality among the brethren.

> Jesus transferred His authority first to the twelve, then to the seventy as a prophetic act of what was to come.

We Are Horizontally Positioned

To believe the gift of leadership is given only to some is to believe there must be an offsetting gift of following that has been given to others. Most people would be uncomfortable making such a statement; however, it is our actions that most clearly demonstrate a doctrine of vertical alignment. While perhaps unintentional, we may find that what we believe collides with how we behave.

What we articulate with our words is never the final judge of our true belief system, but our actions reflect what we claim as truth. A quick inventory of how we relate to others or how we position ourselves with others is all we need to discover whether this vertical alignment lie is at work within our members.[9] The vertically aligned lie is perpetrated by the father of lies and states that there are born leaders and born followers, some born fortunate and some unfortunate, born to be rich or born to be poor, born to be strong or born to be weak. This vertically-aligned lie has penetrated our culture and many of our churches, leading to an illegal leadership structure that limits personal growth. At odds with God's design for promotion, this concept of vertical alignment is hideous in nature. It attempts to either disqualify ourselves or disqualify others. Vertical alignment places limits on sons and daughters and directly contradicts the Father's design for each person.

The leadership truth is that all believers are the salt of the earth, cities on a hill, and the light of the world. This truth is a mandatory recognition that positions us horizontally regardless of position or title. Correctly applied, our horizontal alignment in the kingdom does not *minimize* the importance of authority in our lives but rather *enhances* the importance of authority in our lives. Those in authority lead as Jesus led, celebrate others as Jesus did, and partner with the Holy Spirit as Jesus did in the promoting of others.

---

9 Romans 7:22–23

Identity Is the Key

Recently I walked into Scott's office after our Sunday morning service and collapsed into a mess of sobbing, almost to the point of wailing. I oversee our altar and prophetic ministry teams, and that morning I had become overwhelmed by the "shells" of sons and daughters with whom I had interacted. This ministry time had been much like hunting for live crabs on the beach but finding only empty shells. Many of our sons and daughters have been so robbed of their identity that they reside in a lack of hope and cannot see promises the Father has for them.

The enemy knows that if we do not know who the Father is, we cannot know who we ourselves are. If we do not know who we are, we cannot really know who others are. Without a vibrant and growing heart position that is pursuing God and embracing our true identities, we are left as competitors fighting for scraps.[10] This is the perfect storm for the antichrist spirit to permeate the walls of our hearts and fellowships.

In mainstream Christianity, our true identity as God sees us is under-reported. In Romans 7 Paul writes about the collision between our flesh nature and our spirit man: "For what I will to do, that I do not practice; but what I hate, that I do."[11] It has been too convenient to preach a theology that explains our misbehaviors with a doctrine of we-are-all-just-sinners-saved-by-grace. The problem with any statement identifying us as sinners is that heaven no longer considers us sinners.

The book of Romans does not end with chapter 7. Romans 8:16–17 says, "The Spirit Himself bears witness with our spirit that we are children of God, and if children, then heirs—heirs of God and joint heirs with Christ, if indeed we suffer with Him, that we may also be glorified together." Paul goes on to write in Romans 8:29, "For whom

---

10   Luke 9:46; 22:24

11   Romans 7:15

He foreknew, He also predestined to be conformed to the image of His Son, that He might be the firstborn among many brethren."

Paul immediately provides heaven's answer to the flesh-versus-the-spirit war. That answer is in our identity as developed in the Father and Son's master plan. Far from being identified as just "a sinner saved by grace," our true identity according to heaven is as sons and daughters of the Most High God, joint heirs with Jesus. Paul is simply restating what Jesus said in partnering with the Father in His prayer in John 17:20–23.

> I do not pray for these alone, but also for those who will believe in Me through their word; that they all may be one, as You, Father, are in Me, and I in You; that they also may be one in Us, that the world may believe that You sent Me. And the glory which You gave Me I have given them, that they may be one just as We are one: I in them, and You in Me; that they may be made perfect in one, and that the world may know that You have sent Me, and have loved them as You have loved Me.

Once we are in Jesus, we are no longer identified as sinners but as one in the Godhead. Jesus transferred the glory the Father gave Him to us. This is a key to understanding His promotional plan for our lives.

As identity is key to understanding the Father's plan for us as leaders, intimacy with the Father is the key to identity. It is truly fascinating that the Father leaves few clues to Jesus's childhood development, but what we do know is that by twelve years of age, Jesus had already developed a deeply personal relationship with the Father. No other person had ever referred to God as "My Father."[12]

---

12 Luke 2:49

This level of intimacy was required for Jesus to understand His identity. It is with divine thought that in Jesus's first and last sermons, He taught on intimacy with the Father. Without an innermost craving for constant and permanent placement in the company of the Father, we have an undeveloped identity, and Jesus knew this. To know God is to love Him; to love Him is to abide in Him; and to abide in Him is to know His heart for us and others.

When we abide in Jesus, we discover His identity and, ultimately, our identities.[13] Abiding is "taking every thought captive and making it obedient to Christ"[14]—on steroids. At first, life circumstances are placed on hold as we consider only God's voice. As we mature, abiding develops from a temporary rest stop to a permanent residency. As a love relationship develops, so does a desire to be postured before Him.[15] The position of presenting ourselves before the Father opens a direct conduit between heaven and earth. When we are presented before the Father, other priorities take a back seat.

As our intimacy with the Godhead grows, the inevitable progression is that our identity in Jesus is revealed, embraced, and released. When released into our identities, the true leadership-gifting that God has placed within us blossoms within every son and daughter. Through our raw obedience in being trained and equipped,[16] we are positioned for a life of leadership and promotion as designed by the Author and Owner of promotion.

---

13 John 15

14 2 Corinthians 10:4

15 Romans 12:1

16 Ephesians 4

Chapter 2

Understanding the Title

There is a wonderful exchange in the movie *Braveheart*[1] between William Wallace, a "commoner," and Robert the Bruce, heir to the throne of Scotland. Wallace is leading the fight of freedom for the people of Scotland from the tyrannical and brutal English King Edward the Longshanks. Anxious to keep the status quo and protect his powerbase, The Bruce would not commit to a war of freedom. In a climactic exchange, Wallace challenges Robert the Bruce: "You think the people of this country exist to give you position. I think your position exists to provide those people with freedom, and I go to make sure they have it."[2]

The interaction highlights a disparity in the approach to God's mantle of leadership as portrayed by each character. Robert the Bruce exemplifies one who finds glory in his or her own position. He is an elite, heir-to-the-throne leader, whereas the people are a means to his position. He will do anything to protect his base of power, including aligning with Longshanks. Wallace, however, recognizes that all Scots are elite

---

1 Randall, Wallace. *Braveheart*. Film. Directed by Mel Gibson. Los Angeles: Icon Productions, 1995.

2 Ibid.

and heirs to the throne of the God. Wallace himself is a means to their position.

Jesus needs us to grasp His intent for us to be "salt of the earth" leaders. Our purpose is always to flavor the environment, to connect those around us to God's mercy and grace and lead them to freedom. The maturation process requires our recognition that God's purpose for positions of authority is to help facilitate a connection between Him and His sons and daughters. Because we are already advanced to the highest position available in the kingdom, our titles are provided to advance others into this same sonship.

> The purpose of "salt of the earth" leaders is to flavor the environment.

Mature leaders demonstrate a form of godliness in every action, because they know their promotion was designed for His divine purpose and glory. They carry an internal compass that orients them to the true north purposes of the kingdom. The leadership mantle is not about what we can accomplish or even what our kingdom assignments are. Some of the worst leaders in world history had great accomplishments through conquering people and territory. Also, there have been men and women whom God has called to produce great fruit, but their lack of godly character did not keep up with the assignment, and they ultimately withered. Talent and capacity are traits worthy of possessing, but they alone do not define God's leadership mantle.

God's leadership mantle is placed upon us at birth and develops as we grow into our identities. It is the compilation of the image transfer by God, fully released at the cross and matured by a life of simple and raw obedience. Leadership starts in our hearts, because God first embedded it there.[3] After the Fall, God's ordination of leadership remained. From patriarchs to prophets and from elders to judges, God set in place an

---

3 Genesis 1:26–31

authority structure designed to lead mankind to Him. Ever patient, God's love for us was so great that He even allowed us to be governed in a way He never intended.[4] God's intention for leadership was never for us to lord over and govern others for personal gain but always to be a conduit for connection to Him—never exclusive, always inclusive.

Jesus entered humanity as the Son of Man at the perfect, pre-appointed time. Titled leadership had digressed to an elite powerbase that had to be protected. This has always been illegal and still is today. We will discuss this more in chapter 4. When Jesus was made as a transgressor,[5] He realigned us to our identities as sons and daughters, co-heirs, the light in the world. When Jesus arose, He took His place as Firstborn among many brothers and sisters[6] and positioned us to carry on His work here on earth. Paul realized that Jesus is the example we follow as godly leaders. Paul writes, "Imitate me, just as I imitate Christ."[7] Paul recognized that Jesus provides the blueprint for what was ultimately His transfer of authority, or leadership, to us.

Leadership for Whom?

Leadership positions carry more than the responsibility to lead well. There is an internal process that must take place prior to accepting any title. We must ask this question from the deepest part of our hearts: "For whom are we being promoted?"

If the answer is anything but "For the people with whom we are being asked to serve," then our decisions will reflect that selfish component. Too often, leaders accept positions for personal advancement, financial gain, personal affirmation, or to have authority over others. These

---

4 1 Samuel 8:22

5 Luke 22:35–38

6 Romans 8:29

7 1 Corinthians 11:1

reasons lack understanding of promotion and godly leadership. Ultimately, decisions will be influenced more by personal gain rather than the Holy Spirit-anointed purposes we were designed to fulfill.

When we humbly embrace the Father's purpose in "salt of the earth" leadership, we note a significant uptick in compassion and love for others. Our focus becomes aligned with Jesus's focus. He develops in us the heart of a shepherd. Every word becomes an opportunity to connect people to the love of our Father. Every deed has a purpose. Work of the kingdom takes on a peaceful urgency. We commit to uncommon excellence in all we do. We understand that we will be "deliver[ed] up to councils," and we will be "beaten in the synagogue,"[8] yet our critics have no authority. Our detractors will be unable to undermine His purpose for our lives. Love will be our constant response.

Humility by Trial

When accepting a position of higher authority, have you noticed we can tend to have an air of arrogance? This is especially true of people who have not been beaten up enough by life. There is a degree of validity to the saying "Don't trust a leader who doesn't walk with a limp." Most of us need to get bloodied a bit to understand what leadership is and what leadership is not.

There is a cost to accepting and walking in the leadership mantle, and that cost is our flesh.[9] The more we get promoted, the more we are mandated to live by the Spirit.[10] We can no longer be satisfied with the character flaws, strongholds and sin tendencies gnawing at our members and causing problems with others. We may not be perfect, but we

---

8   Mark 13:9

9   1 Corinthians 15

10   Romans 8

want to walk blamelessly while we are being perfected.[11] The higher the office is, the more public our perfecting becomes. There is a glorious purpose in being perfected publicly. A combination of humility and hunger to be "holy as He is holy"[12] reflects a heart postured to steward our promotion. This is a heart position people will follow if they can visually see it played out.

Inevitably, we will make mistakes. Some mistakes will require simple acknowledgment to correct, and others will require repentance. It is part of the human experience to be so sure we are right about something as to take a hard stance that causes injury to ourselves and others, only to learn, sometimes years later, that we were wrong. Over time, these experiences cause a bit of a limp. The limp reminds us that we are not perfect, our thinking is not perfect, and our theology is not perfect. The limp reminds us that our behavior and speech should reflect to others the same grace that is extended to us.

As an example for us to learn and live by, Jesus was willing to let His disciples learn from mistakes where He could have easily intervened. The most remarkable part of Peter's vision in Acts 10 is not the sheet full of unclean things Jesus used in telling him, "What God has cleansed you must not call [unclean]".[13] I find the most remarkable thing about the story is found in verse 14: "But Peter said, Not so, Lord! For I have never eaten anything common or unclean." Peter had spent three years on earth at Jesus's side, spending nearly every meal with Him. At this point in his life, Peter was willing to say "Not so, Lord!" Such a statement is striking enough, but Jesus's choosing this time to correct thinking He had sanctioned during His three years is remarkable. The eating habits of the Jews were certainly evident during Jesus's time on earth. Why, then, did Jesus not correct that thinking while they were together?

---

11 Philippians 3:12–16

12 Leviticus 20:26; 1 Peter 1:16

13 Acts 10:15

Jesus loves to let us learn some lessons the hard way. He always gives us the opportunity to walk in simple trust and obedience but knows that sometimes the hardness in our hearts needs to be removed with a hard lesson. He knows they are the ones we are least likely to repeat. I can imagine Jesus watching me and with a big smile saying to His entourage, "Let's see if Dave can figure this out on his own." Then when I continue to trip over my own feet, He intervenes with a life circumstance that works as a guide to the revelation He wants me to receive.

Wisdom and Humility Are Partners

Because wisdom and humility are full partners, godly leaders walk in a combination of both that allows them to embrace their servant-leadership position. They are veteran servants long before a title or position is offered. Most often, they are walking in a promotion they themselves have not yet recognized, but others have.

Before I was asked to serve as Executive Director of the iMatter Foundation, I had been refusing pay as a high school coach, preferring instead to donate the thirty hours per week.

> Humility runs from self-promotion and wars against selfish ambition.

I wanted these kids to know I was in it for them, not for the paycheck. I gave to them because they have value and purpose. It was an act of unconditional love, and I received unconditional love in return.

At the time, I did not consider God was watching in admiration. I did not know the blend of His handiwork, and my raw obedience was actually positioning me for promotion. I look back at those days when I turned down Division II college head coaching jobs to work with these kids, and now I can see God was developing in me something

He could work with. Humbly serving Sandy Creek High School in northern New York is among the biggest honors of my life. In many respects, this was a testing ground for my maturity in wisdom and humility.

Humility allows godly leaders to keep their eyes off grandeur and elitism. It runs from self-promotion and wars against selfish ambition. Humility allows us to serve others in unconditional love.

Wisdom advises godly leaders that we cannot do it ourselves. We recognize the need of full partnership with the Holy Spirit and with the people He has sent to do life with us. Wisdom runs from autonomy and wars against selfish, autonomous thoughts. Wisdom tells the mature leader that we were meant to serve in authority and submit under authority with God and man.

Mature leaders understand the mandate to remain postured before the Lord. They refuse to let others rob their personal time with Him. They are not so production-based that the work takes precedence over the Author of the work. They recognize that it is by intentional design a young Joshua is celebrated for remaining behind in the Tabernacle,[14] David encouraged himself in the Lord his God,[15] Daniel fasted and prayed,[16] and Jesus "often went to lonely places and prayed."[17] Our personal assignments include quiet time with Him, taking care of our families, and physical and personal rest. Our corporate assignments also include quiet time with Him, taking care of our families, and physical and personal rest.

---

14 Exodus 33:11

15 1 Samuel 30:6

16 Daniel 10:2–3

17 Luke 5:16

Talk Less; Say More

Mature leaders tend to be the quieter people in the room. They are rarely the first ones offering their advice to a situation; they are less compelled to offer unsolicited opinions. They offer sought-after perspective and counsel. Mature leaders pray daily for wisdom, knowing God will "[give] to all liberally and without reproach."[18]

The books of Proverbs and James provide wonderful insight into God's heart on bridling our tongues and being slow to speak. It is easy to fall in love with our own ideas and agree with everything we've said, but mature leaders have Holy Spirit awareness and know their own wisdom (common sense?) is as foolishness to God.[19] Over time, our own wisdom becomes as folly to ourselves; hence, we are much less willing to offer our own brand of wisdom to others.

A good rule of thumb is that if we are talking more than everyone else, meeting in, meeting out, we may be overly in love with the sound of our own voices or ideas. I have found that the older I get the wiser I get, and the less I talk. Sometimes this is bothersome to others during meetings where ideas are flowing, but I find myself less and less interested in listening to my own dribble.

For some, the challenge of talking less is impossible without setting up some kind of internal game such as "I'm not going to offer perspective in this meeting unless I'm asked" or perhaps even better, "I'm not going to offer my perspective until all others have offered theirs." For others, the challenge is to say more. To become a godly leader requires us to actually become a *leader*. It is not possible to lead by being a monk, unwilling to speak or offer counsel, and this is as strong a self-centered leadership approach as those who dominate every discussion. In truth, it is much easier to train and equip leaders who are bold than to train

---

18 James 1:5

19 1 Corinthians 3:19

leaders who walk in fear or self-loathing doubt. It makes much sense that the disciples we hear from after the resurrection are the disciples we heard from before the resurrection.

Out from Behind the Walls

We are living in the greatest moments in history. A well-publicized and two-decade-long mass exodus out of churches has given way to a hunger building among Jesus's bride. A holy dissatisfaction of the lack of spiritual abundance has been slowly giving way to an all-out passion for passion. At first glance, this exodus appeared as if Jesus's people were checking out. Youth ministries lacked numbers and vigor, church leaders resigned themselves to a lackluster life, and there was a visual lack in spiritual awakening, a lack in finances, and a lack of hope and prosperity.

But Jesus's people were not checking out; they were reconciling with truth, a truth that opens us to the possibility that the Scriptures are for today. There is a new and fresh embracing of Jesus's prayer in Matthew 6:10: "Your Kingdom come. Your will be done on earth as it is in heaven." Thanks in no small part to the raw obedience of apostolic leaders like Bill Johnson (Bethel Church, Redding, California) and Heidi and Roland Baker (Iris Global), there is a massive surge of powerful sons and daughters coming out of the church walls and bringing "this gospel of the kingdom"[20] to a scattered flock.

> Churches are becoming triage centers first, then centers to train, equip, empower, and release street ministers.

---

20   Matthew 24:14

No longer content to focus all effort inside the walls to a shrinking, disenfranchised, and disempowered audience, this new army of "city on a hill" leaders are taking to the streets. Stories about pastors' wives walking the streets shared by prostitutes and demonstrating the Father's unconditional love to them, senior leaders forsaking the comfort of an air-conditioned office to unconditionally love His sons and daughters in Palestinian refugee camps, and business men and women donating half of their income or, even more precious, their time to those under a spirit of addiction are becoming commonplace.

Churches are becoming triage centers first, then centers to train, equip, empower, and release street ministers. The church club is being replaced by a vibrant, loving bride of Christ. If the twentieth century was noted for who or what the church is against, the twenty-first century will be known for who or what the church is for. In the past, church leaders spent most of their time building up the church walls and protecting their own turf, but now, this kingdom age will tear down the walls. Territorialism will be cast down. Denominational factions will dissolve. John 14:11-12 will come alive. Godly leaders will abide in Jesus and have His words abide in them. Anything they desire will be granted.[21]

Paul calls these ideals "the upward calling."

Not that I have already attained, or am already perfected; but I press on, that I may lay hold of that for which Christ Jesus has also laid hold of me. Brethren, I do not count myself to have apprehended; but one thing I do, forgetting those things which are behind and reaching forward to those things which are ahead, I press toward the goal for the prize of the upward call of God in Christ Jesus.

---

21 John 14:13–14; 15:7; 16:23–24

> Therefore let us, as many as are mature, have this mind; and if in anything you think otherwise, God will reveal even this to you. Nevertheless, to the degree that we have already attained, let us walk by the same rule, let us be of the same mind.[22]

Godly leaders will develop great résumés in the kingdom. They will heal the sick, raise the dead, cleanse people with leprosy, and cast out demons.[23] Godly leaders will not be content to read or speak words they do not know how to live by. They will pursue scriptures previously relegated to the shelf. Through a life of abiding and raw obedience, these leaders are positioned for God's promotion.

---

22 Philippians 3:12–16

23 Matthew 10:8

Chapter 3

Author and Owner of Promotion

Our promotion belongs to the Lord. He is the Author and Owner of it. Man is incapable of demoting who God promotes. In fact, man has nothing to do with our promotion.[1] Understanding that our promotion is fully in the jurisdiction of our heavenly Father is the key to unlocking our exponential growth in the body of Christ.

Several years ago I mentored a young youth pastor who struggled with not being promoted after being successful in his role in the church. His frustration had grown to the point that both he and his wife were considering leaving the church and the area to take a position offered by another church. Both husband and wife believed they were not only called by God to the region they currently served in but also called to the church they were youth pastoring in, yet if the senior leadership of the church did not recognize their contributions to the point of promotion, then perhaps it was time to leave.

---

1   Psalm 75:6–7

My young friend had fallen for a popular snare that is set for all of us. The enemy would have us believe our promotion is in the hands of a few stingy leaders, but nothing could be farther from the truth. God is not only the Author of our promotion—He entirely owns it. Man is not capable of promoting us or demoting us. Promotion is God's jurisdiction, not man's. Promotion is the Father's vote of confidence that we are ready for a new level of revelation and understanding. Promotion is always followed by an increase in the wisdom and authority required for us to steward the position. The Father's promotion will enhance our understanding of our identity as well as the identities of the people around us, yet this is counter-intuitive to our observational science. I have preached this truth in the pulpit for years and in our school at Journey University. When I make the statement "God solely authors and owns our promotion, and man is incapable of demoting us," a confused hush comes over the crowd, supplemented by a hint of derision from some veterans.

All of us have experienced the emotional swings of feeling unfairly bypassed by positions or titles or, even more disheartening, being demoted. Without proper perspective, we can develop an approach that can cause us to strive for man's acceptance above God's direction. Improperly understanding who is responsible for our promotion can lead us to work for man's recognition, to obtain position and title. Inevitably, we hit man's ceiling, the height to which man claims we have maximized our skill set and cannot be promoted further.

> Promotion is the Father's vote of confidence that we are ready for a new level of revelation and understanding.

When we embrace the lie that we are being overlooked or bypassed by man, we develop a feeling of rejection that, if left to simmer, will degenerate into hopelessness or disempowerment. This is the position of a stagnant bride, one who lacks vision for God's promotion in her life.

People who lack revelation regarding God's plan for promotion have embraced the lie that man controls their destiny. This fundamental flaw in understanding has a willing accomplice in any leadership structure that more closely resembles a worldly standard than one designed to build and promote the leadership gift the Father places in each of His children. The false structure is born of a misguided philosophy where positions are limited and need to be protected. As senior positions are limited, a selection process fills those limited positions with only the most qualified candidates. This philosophy monitors flock behavior and ties promotion to the outward expression judged to be the most spiritual.

Throughout the last several decades, our churches were attended by unfulfilled sons and daughters. Leadership lived in a constant state of frustration at their lack of ability to "motivate" their flock to greatness. Attendees felt disempowered, and over time, churches declined in numbers and effectiveness. Over those years, I have been in many leadership meetings working to remedy the problem, but to no avail.

In one such meeting, we were reviewing candidates poised for promotion to our eldership team. The starting list was long, though it was quickly whittled down. The leaders inevitably found some disqualifying action or lifestyle for each of the individuals on the list. I was also a participant; my recommendations were disqualified, and I disqualified others' recommendations for a variety of behaviors. As the long list of names narrowed eventually to zero, the inevitable conclusion in the room gravitated to the outcome that there were not enough leaders attending the church. We all agreed to pray for the Lord of the harvest to send the workers.

I have come to realize that we were all missing the point. The Lord of the harvest had done His job; we had not done ours. We had disqualified an entire list of people, some for behavioral issues that were common to the very leadership team doing the disqualifying. In truth, the actions of the assembly were a reflection of an immature leadership team.

God Does Not Wait for Man's Recognition

Most people who are caught up in this church culture have an embedded realization that there is something more than what they are experiencing. That embedded realization comes from the Holy Spirit, who is pressing us to be empowered and released. To grasp our promotion, we must rid ourselves of illegal definitions of what leadership actually is. Too often we consider leadership by terms of titles and positions, but in truth, titles and positions are the result of our demonstrated leadership, the result of our embraced promotion provided by a loving Father who desperately wants His kids to grow up. Our continued growth is enhanced through training and equipping by those in authority over us, but it is not dependent on it. I want to be very clear on this and will cover it in depth in later chapters. People God has placed in authority over us can and should play a decisive role in our training, equipping, empowerment, and release, but if for some reason that is not happening, our maturation depends on our own raw obedience and not others' raw obedience.

The Father's nature wants us all living in the fullness as co-heirs with Jesus. Our God-authored leadership was put in place from the very beginning. As Genesis 1:26–31 says,

> Then God said, "Let Us make man in Our image, according to Our likeness; let them have dominion over the fish of the sea, over the birds of the air, and over the cattle, over all the earth and over every creeping thing that creeps on the earth." So God created man in His own image; in the image of God He created him; male and female He created them. Then God blessed them, and God said to them, "Be fruitful and multiply; fill the earth and subdue it; have dominion over the fish of the sea, over the birds of the air, and over every living thing that moves on the earth."

> And God said, "See, I have given you every herb that yields seed which is on the face of all the earth, and every tree whose fruit yields seed; to you it shall be for food. Also, to every beast of the earth, to every bird of the air, and to everything that creeps on the earth, in which there is life, I have given every green herb for food"; and it was so. Then God saw everything that He had made, and indeed it was very good. So the evening and the morning were the sixth day.

We are all created in image of the Godhead, according to the likeness of the Godhead. We have His compassion, His love, His kindness, His gentleness, His creativity, His passion, all embedded in our DNA. These traits are expressed in different ways and proportions. While sin can and does run interference, it cannot undo what God has done without our partnership.

As God authors and owns our promotion, He has the will and the means to accomplish it. As believers, we are positioned to accept His promotion or to choose to rebel against it regardless of man's acceptance. Our acceptance is predicated by His will and His way; our rebellion delays the outward manifestation of that promotion, which feels like demotion. Others cannot interfere, though they may try. Other people are frequent accomplices to the feeling of being demoted. This is displayed throughout scripture.

Jesus was delivered to Pontius Pilate and, in a single sentence, proved God was the Author and Owner of promotion.

Moses resided in the house of Pharaoh until he was cast out of his homeland for forty years. Promoted by the Lord, he returned to his homeland an outcast and laughing stock. Despite all the might of the strongest empire on earth, God's promotion prevailed.

The Lord also promoted Joseph, yet in immaturity he chose to respond in a spirit of elitism. His brothers were quite willing to help him into the pit.[2] Even still, Joseph responded humbly and faithfully and gained the promised authority. God's promotion prevailed.

Esther, a covert servant, was promoted by God. Through jealousy and deceit, she and her family were sentenced to death by a dictatorial regime, yet she was able to circumvent Haman's genocidal regime and save the people of Israel. God's promotion prevailed.

King Saul was promoted by the Lord and walked in the Spirit of the Lord,[3] yet with his title, he became proud and rebelled against his promotion. Through Saul's refusal of a simple, obedient life, God rejected His own promotion of Saul.

King David was promoted by the Lord, yet the reigning King Saul refused to accept the Lord's promotion. Over a decade of strife, Saul tried to circumvent the Lord's promotion, yet David was trained, equipped, empowered, and then released into the physical manifestation of his promotion. God's promotion prevailed.

Daniel and his friends were teenagers who had no blemishes[4] and were promoted by the Lord. God promoted Daniel to serve as a counselor in and among the most heathen of empires, and Daniel's friends were promoted to serve in the empire. Kings tried to kill them, and sorcerers tried to overthrow them, but God's promotion prevailed.

Jonah, a prophet of God, was also promoted by God. However, he rebelled and fled his assignment. His shipmates were plenty motivated to throw him into the stormy water, even though they feared God's wrath at the act. Jonah repented and was restored to his assignment. God's promotion prevailed.

---

2 Genesis 37

3 1 Samuel 10:6

4 Daniel 1:4

Peter was a fisherman; Matthew was a tax collector; Simon was a zealot; Mary Magdalene was a demon-possessed woman; James and John were eager for title and position; the Samaritan woman was an adulterer; all of these were promoted by God and rejected by man, and God's promotion prevailed.

Judas Iscariot, a self-righteous thief, was promoted by God. Judas rejected his promotion with the willing accomplices of the Sanhedrin. He betrayed the Son of God and carried his rejection to the grave. While man cannot undo our God's promotion, we do have the authority to say, "No" and take that to the grave.

Paul, a self-righteous murderer, was promoted by God and rejected by man, yet he was the scribe in as many as fourteen of the twenty-seven New Testament books. God's promotion prevailed.

Jesus, of a virgin birth, Son of the Most High God, the "us" in Genesis 1:26, the Commander of the army of the Lord of hosts in Joshua 5:14, and was in the furnace with Shadrach, Meshach, and Abed-Nego.[5] He chose to enter the world born as the Lamb sacrifice, taking on himself the eternal penalty of the sin of the world. Man rejected Him; church leadership plotted against Him. Jesus survived multiple attempts on His life until the "appointed hour." He was delivered to Pontius Pilate and in a single sentence proved God was the Author and Owner of promotion: "You could have no power at all against Me unless it had been given you from above."[6] At the appointed time, Jesus went to the cross as remission for our sins, and God's wrath was satisfied. Jesus was crucified, died on the cross, and placed in a tomb. He arose from the dead and now sits at the right hand of God the Father as our intercessor. God's promotion prevailed.

---

5 Daniel 3:25

6 John 19:11

As we are washed in the truth that God the Father authors and owns our promotion, all self-promoting activities cease. We are no longer concerned with whether man recognizes our acts, because we know that our Father does. We do not chase titles or position; our Father works that fully on our behalf. We do not concern ourselves with man's attempts to demote us. Nothing can happen that is not by the Father's hand. Even in times of being in the pit or inside the whale, we recognize these times are corrective acts working out for our and others' good.

We walk in freedom as a son or daughter, knowing that our acts of service provide the documentation that we have accepted our assignment. All the enemy's attempts at self-depredation are eradicated. We are fully persuaded that our heavenly Father has our back. He owns our promotion, which no man can circumvent. The freedom of our promotion is absolute, and no one or nothing can steal it. Old mind-sets that we are being overlooked are cancelled. Any thoughts that others' promotion is taking something away from us are demolished. Every argument that sets itself up against this truth is disregarded. Through taking every thought captive and making it obedient to Jesus,[7] we gain victory over a past of dismissing ourselves and others.

This is a prerequisite to the leadership place we are being promoted to. Until we gain this insight, our actions will be of self-promotion, which kills our spirits and harms others. By definition, self-promotion is self-absorbed. It partners with an illegal spirit of demotion of others. Because it is selfish in nature, it illegally attempts to circumvent God's promotion in His timing. Self-promotion is a sabotuer reflecting a heart set in mistrust in God's handling of our promotion. It represents an impatience with God's training schedule.

God knows what we need to learn and in what areas we need to mature prior to our next promotion. He offers lessons to us on a variety of training schedules from which we can choose. We can learn the first

---

7   2 Corinthians 10

time around or the tenth time around. He is willing to lovingly stay with our stubbornness or release us into the next increase. Ever patient, He will allow us to repeat the same lessons until we learn them. Learning shows maturity and enables our next promotion. God's promotion always means new areas we need to steward. This can feel like a young child going to school for the first time again.

Scott and I have a favorite exchange we repeat at the time of promotion. "How are you today?" one asks.

"In kindergarten again," the other replies.

When we fully adopt the truth that God authors and owns our promotion, all pressure of performance is removed. God is not concerned about what we do; He is focused on who we are and who we become. He knows that when we abide and trust in Him, we live lives of simple and raw obedience. In that place, people around us will hear this gospel of the kingdom from the words we say or the deeds we do. Our predestination to be conformed to the image of Christ[8] will be total and thorough. We walk in authority and under authority. We are positioned for continued promotion.

---

8 Romans 8:29

Chapter 4

Chasing and Hoarding Titles

When we engage in quests for title, position, or promotion, our behavior reflects a belief that God is not the Author of our authority structure. Self-seeking ambition for promotion indicates a belief that somehow God is overlooking us and needs our help to get the ball rolling. Such behavior is incongruent with God's kingdom and closely resembles the world's system.

The world's system is full of dog-eat-dog, rush-to-the-top thinking. These are standard and acceptable practices in the world corporate environment. In the world's corporate system, leaders develop a self-serving approach to chasing titles and hoarding them once achieved. This is a subversive culture of sabotage and passive-aggressive behavior, even amongst supposed allies. Some of the most highly regarded corporations have this dynamic because the corporate system has limitations on numbers of titles and positions. Niche-oriented corporations are designed to fill a narrow set of objectives that place limits on growth potential and positions of authority.

I spent fifteen years with one of America's most successful management firms. The individuals I worked for were among the best quality leaders

I have ever known. Though not practicing Christians, they had a strong people ethic and were kind and compassionate. Hard work was rewarded with compensation enhancement. Although I was promoted quickly, I hit the inevitable ceiling of a corporation with limited vision. There was no opportunity to ascend to the top echelon in the organization. I was never invited into senior leadership. Although I was a top producer, I was rarely asked my opinion on matters that affected my assignment. Because there was a ceiling on my position, there was a ceiling on my growth. I was limited by corporate vision and opportunities for advancement.

Even though the senior leaders desired to create a healthy environment, growth became nearly impossible. Competition among divisions developed. I saw friendships of twenty-plus years disintegrate as leaders vied for the highest offices or positions of authority. What was intended for healthy reliance on each other's talents developed into a dog-eat-dog, self-centered business model. Decisions were influenced by interdivisional rivalry, and the work environment became untenable. As polarization matured, I could no longer rely on other departments for cooperation to accomplish what was supposed to be the corporate vision.

> Titles are never a prelude to leadership; they are a result of demonstrated leadership.

This same dynamic can take place within the church walls and is a demonic strategy. It is inevitable for leaders to develop a drive for attaining titles and recognition from others. This clash of behavior with our true identity is a primary strategy of the enemy. The biggest threat to Satan's empire is sons and daughters walking in the fullness of their identities. If he can get us "fighting over the scraps of Longshanks table,"[1] we will walk in constant competition because of our need for affirmation and drive for

---

1 Randall, Wallace. *Braveheart*. Film. Directed by Mel Gibson. Los Angeles: Icon Productions, 1995.

position. People who have title strive to keep it, and those who want title strive to take it.

Titles are never a prelude to leadership, because they are a result of demonstrated leadership. Position should never be used as a divider or a place of separation but as a unifier. Jesus condemned titled church leadership with His strongest language when those titles were used as a separation between, instead of a connection to, His sons and daughters. In truth, God demands the flock from the hands of self-serving shepherds. When we use titles of apostles, prophets, teachers, pastors, and evangelists, in any form, to advance our personal position, we are at risk of being adversarial to the Lord of Hosts.

Consider what God says in Ezekiel 34:1–11:

> And the word of the LORD came to me, saying, "Son of man, prophesy against the shepherds of Israel, prophesy and say to them, 'Thus says the LORD GOD to the shepherds: "Woe to the shepherds of Israel who feed themselves! Should not the shepherds feed the flocks? You eat the fat and clothe yourselves with the wool; you slaughter the fatlings, **but** you do not feed the flock. The weak you have not strengthened, nor have you healed those who were sick, nor bound up the broken, nor brought back what was driven away, nor sought what was lost; but with force and cruelty you have ruled them. So they were scattered because **there was** no shepherd; and they became food for all the beasts of the field when they were scattered. My sheep wandered through all the mountains, and on every high hill; yes, My flock was scattered over the whole face of the earth, and no one was seeking or searching **for them**."
>
> 'Therefore, you shepherds, hear the word of the LORD: "**As I** live," says the LORD GOD, "surely because My flock became a

prey, and My flock became food for every beast of the field, because *there was* no shepherd, nor did My shepherds search for My flock, but the shepherds fed themselves and did not feed My flock"— therefore, O shepherds, hear the word of the LORD! Thus says the LORD GOD: "Behold, I *am* against the shepherds, and I will require My flock at their hand; I will cause them to cease feeding the sheep, and the shepherds shall feed themselves no more; for I will deliver My flock from their mouths, that they may no longer be food for them."

'For thus says the LORD GOD: "Indeed I Myself will search for My sheep and seek them out."'

It is important to note the Lord was speaking to "His" shepherds. These were chosen leaders selected for the purpose of caring for Father God's flock, yet their motivations were not solely dedicated to care for the flock. They were dominated by selfish ambition.

In Matthew 23 Jesus addressed the very same dynamic with the leaders during His time on earth:

Then Jesus spoke to the multitudes and to His disciples, saying: "The scribes and the Pharisees sit in Moses' seat. Therefore whatever they tell you to observe, that observe and do, but do not do according to their works; for they say, and do not do. For they bind heavy burdens, hard to bear, and lay them on men's shoulders, but they themselves will not move them with one of their fingers. But all their works they do to be seen by men. They make their phylacteries broad and enlarge the borders of their garments. They love the best places at feast, the best seats at the synagogues, greetings in the market-places, and to be called by men, 'Rabbi, Rabbi.' But you, do not be called 'Rabbi'; for One is your Teacher, the Christ and you are all brethren. Do not call anyone on earth your father, for One is your Father, He who is in heaven. And do not be called teachers, for One is your Teacher, the Christ. But he who is greatest among you shall be your servant. And whoever exalts himself will be humbled, and he who humbles himself will be exalted."[2]

There are startling components in Jesus's words here. Although His words were delivered just two days before He went to the cross, He reminds us that the scribes and the Pharisees "sit in Moses' seat. Therefore, whatever they tell you to observe, that observe and do."

This remarkable command was given to both the multitudes and the disciples. I wonder what the disciples thought after being lumped in with the multitudes and told to observe what the Pharisees told them to observe. Though they were given this honorable place in Jesus' life, as one of the twelve, they still were held to a standard of "He who is greatest among you shall be your servant."

What must have Peter, James, and John thought? "Lord, I thought you said you were going to build your church on me." "Surely I have a high-honor position and should be treated with the utmost of respect by the people." "Surely I've earned the best seat at the feasts and the synagogue."

Jesus is greatly attracted to the humble in spirit to the point that He commands us to be so. He is clear in His instructions to avoid getting caught up in titles,[3] and He became the standard for whom He promotes and why. Jesus bestows great favor on people who utilize

---

2   Matthew 23:1–12

3   Matthew 23:7

their promotion in title and position to feed His sheep. People who lord over and self-indulge are adversarial to the Father's heart.

Anything that separates us has the potential to divide us. This is especially true when we focus on titles and positions. Jesus directly points this out when criticizing the Pharisees who loved to be called "Rabbi, Rabbi." That was His very reason in saying it twice. "Look at me; look at me." Jesus's criticism was designed not to undermine godly, authoritative structure but to remind those in authority of their true purpose.

> Anything that separates us has the potential to divide us.

People who carry the promotion and authority of the Father do not need to remind their "subjects" of their title. I have noted that every time I get caught up in telling people what my title is, it is because I am not secure in that position. Over the years I see many of God's appointed leaders often declare, "I'm the director of this," or "I'm in charge of that." It is nothing but a mentality of selfish ambition: *I, I, I, me, me, me.*

At Journey Center we conduct an annual conference called Accelerant. Every year we bring in national speakers and prophetic leaders to complement the abundance of leadership talent in our house. In 2016 we had Jack Taylor, Kris Vallotton, Bill Vanderbush, Charlie Coker, and others. I overheard a comment made by one of these men toward our senior leader Scott Lowmaster. He said, "I've been here for three days, and if I didn't know who you were, I wouldn't know you were the senior leader." Scott is an amazing servant. While he had a reserved seat in the front row, he was rarely there. He simply served alongside the amazing people in our fellowship, the wonderful sons and daughters who may not carry a big title but walk in the promotion of the Lord.

As the prophetic oversight of the house, I steward impartation opportunities as they arise. I have been to many otherwise excellent conferences where speakers spend more time affirming and imparting to each other than to the wonderful sons and daughters who do not have reserved seating. At Accelerant, we are intentional about keeping the reserved seats necessary for logistics, but not in the best seats in the house. Our front and center rows are open seating. This is not a braggadocios statement but recognition that Jesus quite intentionally promotes us to "feed My lambs," "tend My sheep," and "feed My sheep."[4]

> In the kingdom, all positions are purposed for serving His precious children.

In God's kingdom, all positions are purposed for serving His precious children.[5] There are no elite titles established for any other cause than "we all come to the unity of the faith, and of the knowledge of the Son of God, to a perfect man, to the measure of the stature of the fullness of Christ . . . speaking the truth in love, [that we] may grow up in all things into Him who is the Head—Christ."[6] Contrary to the corporate paradigm of limited positions of authority, each person in God's kingdom has access to the high calling in Christ Jesus.[7] God raises up apostles, prophets, evangelists, pastors, and teachers in His timing and for His reasoning. It is good to seek these things[8] but important we do not derail God's timing for ourselves or others.

People walking in this truth are incapable of hoarding positions. They recognize that growth is incumbent with promotion. Consider the following common journey within the church. Senior leaders train and equip young leaders to take different roles within the church, such as youth pastors. True to the kingdom model, through mentorship,

---

4 John 21:15–17

5 Ephesians 4:11–16

6 Ephesians 4:13-15

7 Philippians 3:14

8 1 Timothy 3:1

the youth ministry grows. As the youth pastors mature, they, too, train and equip their subordinates. At an appointed time, the Father promotes the youth pastors to a new assignment, perhaps as a teacher, evangelist, prophet or apostle. As the youth pastors are promoted, it is a joyous transition where new youth ministry leaders are appointed and anointed into their new assignment.

This journey is repeated throughout the kingdom positions. In the kingdom, promotion begets promotion. As we mature, it is our joy to partner with the Father's heart of promotion. As commonly stated, our ceiling is our "disciples" floor.[9]

---

9 John 14:11–12

Section 2

ATTRIBUTES OF A GODLY LEADER

Chapter 5

Character Matters

A developed and intentional godly character is a primary positioner for our promotion. People do not follow titles; they follow character. Effective leadership requires a strong code of ethics and integrity. The higher we climb in position or promotion, the more eyes are upon us. Moral failures become public exhibitions,[1] but Father God knows that as He promotes His elect, it is His name that is being promoted.

Character is an outward expression of our internal moral compass. It is the mechanism that prevents or allows unrighteous behavior. Our character is measured by our commitment to righteousness and holiness in everyday life. As we mature, the Holy Spirit challenges us to a high standard of righteousness. He is faithful to confront self-preservation behaviors that cause us to cut corners in holiness, and our character is on display in how we communicate and treat others and how we behave when no one is watching.

One of my friends is the senior executive of a large corporation and likes to take prospective management candidates out to dinner. He

---

1 Luke 12:1–3

observes how they order their food, how polite and complementary they are to the wait staff, their manners while eating, alcohol intake levels, and overall demeanor while in the company of others. He recognizes character is on display in how we interact with others, especially others we may feel are our subordinates. I have heard of others who would take golfers out for a round of golf during the hiring process to observe how prospective candidates score their round or respond to bad shots or holes.

> Character is an outward expression of our internal moral compass.

Senior executives recognize that all their staff are reflections of them and the company they work for. God knows that, too. He knows titles alone will not produce lasting fruit or build loyal teams. At best, subordinates will do what titles tell them to do and then only when purposes are aligned. As long as titles provide benefits such as pay, position, or increased influence, titles alone may obtain some level of cooperation. However, titles unaccompanied by godly character will never obtain loyalty and unity. This is true in every corporate, team, or church setting. I have witnessed many talented men and women who have great capacities in their professions or lives but endlessly struggle with their staff and associates due to a lack of godly character.

Conversely, I have known many who do not profess Christianity who demonstrate great godly character and hence have developed work environments that highlight honor, acknowledgment, and promotion. This dynamic can be observed in any retail store. Work atmosphere is a clear indicator of the level of character of the senior leadership. Those who are self-aware enough to intentionally commit to kindness, honor, acknowledgment, and promotion will inevitably have a healthier atmosphere than those who cut corners with their integrity.

Leadership is best demonstrated when led from the front. Up-front leaders are always on display, and their character is the prototype for others to follow. Godly character begets godly character in those with whom we are positioned to lead. A prerequisite for godly leadership is how we respond to poor behavior from others. At Journey Center, a continual thread in our discussions is how we respond to poor behavior in others. One of our favorite sayings is "Others' poor behavior does not legalize poor behavior in us."

Uriah is one of my favorite Bible heroes. In all the stories and writings of David and his mighty men, his generals, and their exploits, none was equal to that of Uriah. Uriah sacrificed everything to his king and his people—everything but his character.[2] That was something that even King David could not have. When David tried to bring Uriah into his scheme to cover his sin, Uriah's internal compass would have none of it. Uriah gave his life before succumbing to unrighteousness.

Demonstrating godly character is easy while we are in a lovefest of success. Our character is tested by trials. Godly character is best displayed during such difficulties as when we are mistreated, when our finances are on empty, or when we are having a tough day emotionally. Men and women of godly character have learned trials are opportunities. Paul puts it this way:

> Godly character is best displayed during difficulties.

> Therefore, having been justified by faith, we have peace with God through our Lord Jesus Christ, through whom also we have access by faith into this grace in which we stand, and rejoice in hope of the glory of God. And not only that, but we also glory in tribulations, knowing that tribulation produces perseverance; and perseverance, character; and character, hope.[3]

---

2 2 Samuel 11:11

3 Romans 5:1–4.

Our personal power statements affirm godly character, but unfortunately the sinful nature of our flesh as well. Positive power statements displayed by our deeds promote an atmosphere of trust and unity, while negative power statements backed up by our deeds promote distrust and disunity.

Four Common Power Statements

Positive Power Statement: *We are all in this together.*

Jesus was brilliant at inviting everyone to His high position. It showed a character trait of being totally self-aware of who He was and also a great hunger for unity with us. He was purposeful to remove any illegal powerbase or faction. He opened the club to women, lepers, adulterers, thieves, and braggarts. Just before His death, he brought total clarity to our joint position as co-heirs. John 17:20–23 shows Jesus promoting us as co-heirs:

> I do not pray for these alone, but also for those who will believe in Me through their word; that they all may be one, as You, Father, are in Me, and I in You; that they also may be one in Us, that the world may believe that You sent Me. And the glory which You gave Me I have given them, that they may be one just as We are one: I in them, and You in Me; that they may be made perfect in one, and that the world may know that You have sent Me, and have loved them as You have loved Me.

Great leaders have an innate ability to raise others up to their position instead of relegating themselves to a high position to keep others down. It is remarkable that the Son of the Most High God was interested in raising us up to His position. This is a trait He wants us to closely mimic. He wants us to carry His heart of promotion and recognize the glory of God He has placed in others.

Godly character always guards against being lofty in our own eyes.[4] I have counselled many young people who fell into a form of personal pride after promotion. They were frustrated in areas that hinted they were in self-promotion mode. Some were frustrated at a lack of cooperation from subordinates or peers, and some where frustrated that though they carried a title, they were not consulted on several decisions. I graciously pointed out how entitlement had crept into their thinking. Holding ourselves more highly than we ought creates in us an expectation of more advancement versus allowing God to author our promotion. We need to be vigilant toward subtle attitudes of entitlement or superiority to ensure that they do not creep into our thinking.[5]

Prideful exhibitions are a real danger point when we are promoted.[6] Satan's character is one of pride, and it is a key tool he effectively uses to ensnare us. Satan is lofty in his own eyes. He took his promotion as his own greatness and over time rebelled haughtily against the Lord. When we are promoted, Satan attempts to impart that same prideful, haughty, rebellious attitude into us.

We counter that by understanding that we are all on a level playing field. When we are promoted, the low road is the highway to godly character. We can simultaneously be confident and thankful in our position and remain humble enough to recognize when we are indeed in over our heads. Jesus rarely told people who He was. His godly character was fully matured. Mature leaders develop character that does not require recognition from others in order for them to lead. They recognize that godly authority is placed on earth for our benefit.

---

4   Romans 12:3

5   Jeremiah 9:23–24

6   Genesis 37:5–7

Mature leaders also recognize that titles are not meant to divide but instead to unite in purpose and destiny. After all, our role is to raise up others.

Negative Power Statement: *Nice guys finish last.*

This is among the most moronic statements I have ever heard, and it is difficult to comprehend how such a statement could make it into the mainstream. The basis of this belief is "If I demonstrate kindness, then I'll be taken advantage of and therefore will not accomplish my or the corporate goals and objectives." This belief puts us at enmity with God and man. Graham Cooke writes and speaks about how God is the "kindest person he has ever known." Graham is right. Kindness is a prevailing character trait of our heavenly Father. Everything He does is done out of perfect knowledge and love for His children. Every written and unwritten action of our Father is based out of His lovingkindness. He is constantly on the prowl for intimacy and to restore us for the purpose of intimacy with Him. Kindness is in God's image. It is demonstrated in His Spirit.[7] We, being made in the image of the Godhead, have kindness embedded in our DNA. We are predestined to be conformed back to His image.[8]

The opposite of kindness is cruelty. Every unkind word or act is by definition cruel.[9] If we only knew the devastating effect an unkind word or act has on those around us. We are surrounded by sons and daughters who hunger for affirmation. We all seek it, and while it can be truly found only in the Father through the Son, we all have the great honor to be, as Bob Sorge puts it, the best man/maid of honor at the wedding ceremony.

---

7 Galatians 5:22

8 Romans 8:29

9 Ezekiel 34:4

The "Nice guys finish last" belief system puts us at enmity with our subordinates, partners, and authority figures. A lack of kindness undermines efforts to accomplish corporate goals and objectives. It creates an environment where passive-aggressive behavior is sure to show up, even in those who are passive-aggressive adverse. Passive-aggressive behavior is a saboteur. It refuses unity at key times in an effort to undermine success. When we walk in kindness, people root for us; when we walk in unkindness, people root against us.

Positive Power Statement: I'm sorry. I was wrong.

A leader who is willing to admit mistakes is a leader who promotes a culture of trust. Mistakes are not failures until we try to cover them up. I have personally struggled in this area. I suppose it is a reflection of many years of feeling like a failure, but in the maturation process, I have discovered that admitting my mistakes has been difficult for me.

A heartfelt apology exhibits remorse for causing a painful situation. It demonstrates to the people around us that we do not consider ourselves beyond reproach. This is not a "falling on our own sword" act of martyrdom; rather, it is a genuine recognition of the pain or inconvenience our words and actions caused to others. It is important that accompanying an apology is a required change of approach. Sometimes we are faced with a personal stronghold that has us entrenched in counter-productive behaviors, so this apology may need to be repeated a few times. However, with persistent commitment to heart change, subordinates and peers will have tremendous grace for a leader who is actively working to correct a character flaw. In truth, the admiration for such a leader will develop into great loyalty toward that leader.

We need to be cautious to avoid providing non-apologetic substitutes. Statements like "I'm sorry if I hurt you, but . . ." then listing the reason we were coerced into the mistake are not remorse but an accusation that insinuates, "You made me hurt you." I am always wary when someone starts a sentence with "I'm sorry, but . . ." To date, I have yet to note any remorse coming after the "but." It is a gateway to stating another person's failure.

Humility is a powerful weapon and fully partnered with wisdom. Without humility, wisdom is useless, for all wisdom comes from God. A leader who is humble enough to admit his or her mistakes, repent of sinful actions, and learn and grow in godly character is a leader the Lord can bestow great wisdom unto.

Negative Power Statement: *The end justifies the means.*

By uttering this statement, we are saying it does not matter how we accomplish the goal as long as we accomplish it. I have known many corporate leaders who demonstrate this philosophy, leaders who will do whatever it takes and say whatever they need to say to coerce people to serve their needs. Such "leaders" behave as if they are above the law. They believe that because their cause is so great, they can cut corners. Commonly, they will disobey traffic laws, cut ethical financial corners, and dispense with common courtesy because their belief system says their mission is more important than these "surface" character traits.

This philosophy puts our character up for sale. King Saul is the poster child for cutting the corners of good character. His reign as king over Israel was shortened because of this tendency. In his arrogance, he broke rule after rule. He unlawfully gave a sacrifice;[10] he made foolish boasts;[11] he kept what he was to give and gave what he was to keep;[12] he caused his staff to be afraid of him;[13] he did not accompany his

---

10   1 Samuel 13

11   1 Samuel 14

12   1 Samuel 15

13   1 Samuel 16

men in battle;[14] he became jealous of his subordinates;[15] and he threw public jabs with spears at one of his most loyal staff members.[16] Do you see a negative pattern? Saul considered himself above the law. He made foolish boasts he could not back up, and he became paranoid about a young protégé taking his title. He told his versions of the truth instead of the truth.

> In the kingdom, how we arrive is where we arrive in terms of completing our assignments.

Before forming my own company, I worked twenty-five years in the corporate setting. Often I saw supervisors tell "white lies" to clients, staff, and each other, which was frightening. White lies are lies. Intentionally leaving out key information to sway opinions in favor of ours is a lie, and half-truths are not truths. It is an "ends justify the means" mind-set that reveals a lack of godly character. When one of my supervisors made decisions he knew he should consult others about, he would say, "It's better to ask forgiveness than permission." There are two lies in that statement. Lie one is "I'm asking forgiveness" and lie two is "I don't need wise counsel."

In the kingdom, how we arrive is where we arrive in terms of completing our assignments. Our true character shows up in word and deed.[17] How we arrive will have a massive impact on where we arrive. Jesus provided the ultimate example and issued strong warnings about our early conduct in Matthew 24–27. The word of our testimony is how we overcome the accuser of the brethren.[18] Uncompromising godly character keeps us blameless before God and man.

---

14 1 Samuel 17

15 1 Samuel 18

16 1 Samuel 19

17 John 14:11

18 Revelation 12:11

Chapter 6

Acknowledgment Matters

One of the fundamentals at iMatter initiative is that every son and daughter deserves eye contact and a smile. This simple act is the first step in recognizing and celebrating God's handiwork in others. When we take a moment to make eye contact and smile, our spirit is telling their spirit they matter. We are telling them plainly and directly that we see a value and purpose worth acknowledging and that they are a pleasure to us. We are telling them they are welcome in our space and in our lives. This simple act of kindness has an important impact on us and those around us. When we make eye contact and smile, our countenance expresses His countenance, which states, "I'm pleased with you."[1] Our countenance is the welcome mat to our heart.

This is a difficult thing to do at times. I tend to posture myself before the Lord, which at times can feel like a deep trance. I have learned to do it throughout the day and can go about my work while being postured. However, I can become so focused on listening to the Lord that I am unaware of my surroundings, and I can have a very stern

---

1 Matthew 17:5

look on my face. The deeper I am listening, the sterner I look. My inner man is at peace and rejoicing as I'm communing with the Holy Spirit and focused on hearing prophetically from Him, but the people looking at me sometimes wonder what's the matter with me and why I look so intense.

> Every son and daughter deserves
> eye contact and a smile.

As I have been promoted by the Lord to more senior positions, my station has been increasingly visible and public. As a prophet of the Lord, speaker, worshiper, and father figure, the amplified prominence causes more and more people being tuned into my countenance. Hence, the stern countenance has to vacate. I now have "face police" around me. Lisa Lowmaster started this concept, and believe me when I say that it is quite challenging. When Lisa notices a stern countenance on my face, she simply looks at me with a smile and says, "Face." I admit to not really enjoying it. It tends to ruin my peace and cause me to actually feel stern, yet I am thankful Lisa loves me and others enough to be bold for God's kingdom. She knows my heart and knows I would not want others to feel unwelcome around me because I have not learned to train my countenance into a kind expression.

This has helped me be aware of my surroundings while walking in the Spirit, a lesson I may not have learned otherwise if Lisa and others had not helped me realize it. When we train our countenances to be welcoming, we are training our spirits to be aligned with Jesus's spirit.[2] Jesus's countenance drew others to Him. He was warm and welcoming. I believe He smiled easily.

---

2 2 Corinthians 4:6

Praising Others

One of the things I most admire about Scott Lowmaster, senior leader at the Journey Center, is that he is always ready with an encouraging word. Scott recognizes we all need to feel valued and appreciated. Mark Twain once said, "I can live for two months on a good compliment." I would have to agree with Mr. Twain.

Before we get too hung up in religious thinking, remember what the definition of "praise" is. According to *Webster's*, praise means "to say or write good things about someone or something; to express approval about someone or something."[3] This is not worshiping the created versus the Creator; it is acknowledging and praising His handiwork. Receiving the praise of others builds our self-esteem. It makes us feel recognized, accepted, and respected. A word of timely praise can be a launching point in one's desire to grow and mature. Heartfelt praise from others, especially from those we look up to, is prophetic affirmation that we are on the right path.

The gift of prophecy has a primary purpose to edify, encourage, and comfort. Paul's exhortation in 1 Corinthians 14:1–3 is that all should prophesy: "Pursue love, and desire spiritual gifts, but especially that you may prophesy. For he who speaks in a tongue does not speak to men but to God, for no one understands him, however, in the spirit he speaks mysteries. But he who prophesies speaks edification and exhortation and comfort to men." Mature leaders make targeted and personal encouragement part of their intentional duties, and it is indeed our duty.[4] When we praise others, we walk in agreement with all God has done in and through the target of our praise. We declare what God is doing is a good thing and worthy to be praised. We are commending His handiwork.

---

3 "praise," Merriam-Webster. https://www.merriam-webster.com/dictionary/praise

4 Romans 12:6–16

I believe a desire to feel praise is implanted by our heavenly Father, which is part of His image transfer in Genesis 2:26. God is remarkably effective at recognizing the good in Himself, in others, and in all He has created. He does not have an ego that needs stroking; He is absolute truth and so declares absolute truth. He does not fear that praise or worship will somehow ruin Him or that he would lose His righteousness or holiness. God is intentional about declaring His handiwork good to the extent He made His attributes clearly made known to all mankind.[5]

God loves to brag on us, too, and He does it openly and loudly. We are His workmanship. The example in Job is magnificent;[6] the fact that we make His heart beat is incredible;[7] His desire to lavish us with gifts is mindboggling,[8] and His intention to have nothing separate us from Him is proof of His eternal optimism regarding us.[9]

Jesus was equally intentional in praising others. He openly praised Nathanial for His honesty;[10] He praised John the Baptist as the greatest prophet to ever live;[11] He publicly marveled about the centurion's faith;[12] He praised the woman who wept on His feet and dried her tears with her hair;[13]

> God wants us to feel His admiration for our simple acts of obedience.

---

5 Romans 1:20

6 Job 1:8

7 Song of Solomon 4:9

8 1 Corinthians 13; James 1:17

9 Romans 8:38–39

10 John 1:47

11 Matthew 11:11

12 Matthew 8:10

13 Luke 7:44–47

He honored the widow for her extravagant gift;[14] He praised Mary for anointing His feet,[15] and He praises us in the throne room now.[16]

The Godhead does not seem too worried about all this praise opening us up for pride and arrogance. Instead, God wants us to feel His admiration for our simple acts of obedience. Consider how Jesus openly praised the Roman centurion for his faith in Matthew 8:5–10:

> Now when Jesus had entered Capernaum, a centurion came to Him, pleading with Him, saying, "Lord, my servant is lying at home paralyzed, dreadfully tormented." And Jesus said to him, "I will come and heal him." The centurion answered and said, "Lord, I am not worthy that You should come under my roof. But only speak a word, and my servant will be healed. For I also am a man under authority, having soldiers under me. And I say to this one, 'Go,' and he goes; and to another, 'Come,' and he comes; and to my servant, 'Do this,' and he does it." When Jesus heard it, He marveled, and said to those who followed, "Assuredly, I say to you, I have not found such great faith, not even in Israel!"

If our heavenly Father openly praises us, why would we be stingy with our praises of others? We should be on guard for selfish ambition when we withhold our praise of others. Satan would have us believe that if we acknowledge others, it somehow diminishes us. This directly contradicts God's heart. Psalms 50:23 says, "Whoever offers praise glorifies Me; and to him who orders his conduct aright I will show the salvation of God." Far from diminishing us, praising others glorifies God.

---

14 Luke 21:3-4

15 Mark 14:9

16 Romans 8:34

When we are generous with our praise, it tells God that He can entrust us with His kids and positions us for promotion. He notes that our hearts are focused on empowering those around us through recognizing their good deeds. To openly praise others is part of a leader's requirement in training and equipping others into their assignments. Public praise counters and removes the critical spirit others have about themselves. God promotes us to both coach and cheer others to develop and to promote their God-given true identity.

Elijah's Cave

Over the years I have fallen into the trap of "As long as I receive the affirmation from Jesus, I'm okay" and somehow convince myself that I do not need to hear affirmation from those I live with, yet every time this occurs, I find myself whining in this inner cave. Like Elijah, I hear the "I'm all alone" lie. The Lord's response is comical . . . unless you are in the cave. I envision Him with a big smile on His face as He listens to me whine, all the while noting all the wonderful sons and daughters He has surrounded me with. Eventually, God gets around to reminding me He will not be found in that whining place. Like with Elijah, He directly tells me to quit whining; He has not left me alone, and I need to get up and get back to doing my work.[17]

Satan is motivated to try to get us feeling alone. If he can get us alone, he can pick us off. If his attacks are left unchallenged, we will move toward isolation. God knows this is unhealthy behavior. Ecclesiastes 4:9–12 says,

> Two are better than one,
> Because they have a good reward for their labor.
> For if they fall, one will lift up his companion.
> But woe to him who is alone when he falls,

---

17   1 Kings 19:13–18

For he has no one to help him up.
Again, if two lie down together, they will keep warm;
But how can one be warm alone?
Though one may be overpowered by another, two can withstand him.
And a threefold cord is not quickly broken.

God did not create us to live life alone in a cave without affirmation and encouragement from others. He has surrounded us with His brilliant sons and daughters, a point Jesus was intentional to demonstrate throughout Scripture. He could balance His alone time with the Father as well as the demands of full-time ministry. Jesus never robbed the Father of His intimate time, nor did He forsake friendship and fellowship. He was always enlarging His group. I believe even the celebrated Big Three, Peter, James and John, grew to include Mary Magdalene and Jesus's mother.

Isolation is never a pathway to encouraging others. I have yet to meet a person who is an encourager and living in isolation. Isolationists choose to wall themselves off frequently because they do not see the good in themselves, so they cannot see the good in others. Isolation leaves us to hear the accuser telling us what we are not and what others are not. Satan is happy to heap on guilt and shame, but God's plan is that through community we walk in the fullness of our identities as sons and daughters. Leaders living in God's promotion recognize the need for freely receiving and offering frequent encouragement and praise to others.

> Isolation is never a pathway to encouraging others.

Generous Speech

There are dozens of scriptures commanding us to encourage one another, yet without a deep understanding of the power of the tongue, encouragement will remain an elusive or inadequate part of our daily routines. Proverbs 18:21 proclaims, "Death and life are in the power of the tongue." This is true at the deepest levels in the spirit world. We partner with the spirit of life or the spirit of death with each of our words. A word of encouragement lifts others up into life, while a word of condemnation can bring death into their lives.

Likewise, James 3 pulls no punches:

> My brethren, let not many of you become teachers, knowing that we shall receive a stricter judgment. For we all stumble in many things. If anyone does not stumble in word, he is a perfect man, able also to bridle the whole body. Indeed, we put bits in horses' mouths that they may obey us, and we turn their whole body. Look also at ships: although they are so large and are driven by fierce winds, they are turned by a very small rudder wherever the pilot desires. Even so the tongue is a little member and boasts great things.
>
> See how great a forest a little fire kindles! And the tongue is a fire, a world of iniquity. The tongue is so set among our members that it defiles the whole body, and sets on fire the course of nature; and it is set on fire by hell. For every kind of beast and bird, of reptile and creature of the sea, is tamed and has been tamed by mankind. But no man can tame the tongue. It is an unruly evil, full of deadly poison. With it we bless our God and Father, and with it we curse men, who have been made in the similitude of God. Out of the same mouth proceed blessing and cursing. My

brethren, these things ought not to be so. Does a spring send forth fresh water and bitter from the same opening? Can a fig tree, my brethren, bear olives, or a grapevine bear figs? Thus no spring yields both salt water and fresh

Who is wise and understanding among you? Let him show by good conduct that his works are done in the meekness of wisdom. But if you have bitter envy and self-seeking in your hearts, do not boast and lie against the truth. This wisdom does not descend from above, but is earthly, sensual, demonic. For where envy and self-seeking exist, confusion and every evil thing are there. But the wisdom that is from above is first pure, then peaceable, gentle, willing to yield, full of mercy and good fruits, without partiality and without hypocrisy. Now the fruit of righteousness is sown in peace by those who make peace.

James provides excellent exhortation and words of danger for those being promoted in the Lord. It would be a contradiction to say Jesus is suggesting we do not become teachers. Instead, James is cautioning us not to accept a promotion from man prematurely, especially before we have learned to bridle our tongue.

When providing praise and encouragement to others, the guidelines of wisdom in verse 17 are brilliant. Note the warning against providing praise with partiality and hypocrisy. We need to use caution not to advance our own positions with praise targeted to those who can advance us expressly for that purpose. Our leaders need encouragement, so let us do it with a pure heart.

Mature leaders praise without partiality and without being condescending. When we praise the people in authority over us, we do it from pure hearts to recognize God's manifested greatness. When we praise those we are in a level of authority over, we praise them as equals with the intent of raising them up. A leader who has a developed life of praise and encouraging others will be promoted to a level of entrusted authority. From this place, our promoted authority is positioned to partner with the Holy Spirit to love, train, equip, empower, and release others into their destinies.

Chapter 7

Becoming A Great Coach

Strong leaders are great coaches. As we mature, it is important to develop our coaching styles and habits so we can maximize the return on our promotion.[1] In twenty-seven years of coaching college and high school varsity basketball and football, I studied many head and assistant coaches. I continually observed what other coaches did well and what pitfalls they frequented.

I am not an ingenious person by nature. If it were up to me, rocks and sticks would still be our tools of war. I may have thought to sharpen a stick at some point, but any further inventions like steel and gunpower would not have come from me, but what I do well is study and learn from others. Because I am not afraid to learn from others, my arsenal is deep and wide as I adopt and improve on what others have done. Whether through a gift of creativity or of hard work, we all can become great coaches.

There are three primary traits that separate great coaches from the rest:

---

1 Matthew 25:14–30

1. They recognize good ideas when they hear them.

2. They recognize their team contributions over their own.

3. They are confident and know the source of their confidence.

Great Coaches Know Good Ideas When They Hear Them

In coaching over one thousand games, I have been part of many wins against coaches and players who were stuck in antiquated behaviors and systems. Stubbornly adhering to practices that produce failure will ultimately produce failure. This kind of self-indulgence creates an environment of blaming others for the loss. Coaches blame officials or their players, and players point fingers at other players or coaches. Instead of recognizing their limitations and maturing or updating their approaches, teams become predictable and stagnant. This trend can continue for years. These coaches tend to be angry most of the time. They blame their schools, their athletic directors, or even the generation of players.

Meanwhile, the primary culprit is the coaching staff who are unwilling to grow and mature. I have coached at the high school level and beaten the same teams every time for ten years straight. I saw the same offenses and defenses, the same player tendencies, the same use of the clock, the same application of the rules. This is not unique to athletics. Corporate and ministry leaders need to guard against this same dynamic. Mature leaders are teachable people. They recognize that failure to learn creates a pool of stagnant water, mold, and mosquitoes. It is not a productive mind-set toward success.

Mature leaders are teachable people.

As I coached, my teams frequently won, not because we had more talented players but because we as coaches recognized that team success was directly tied to player success, and we would recruit and utilize any legal tool we could find to develop and promote our players. We studied and trained ourselves before training our players. We were on a constant hunt for the next great idea that would make us better, and we did not care if it came from inside or outside the staff. Players frequently gave great us great insight.

The late Dean Smith, long-time head coach of the North Carolina Tar Heels men's varsity basketball team, wrote a marvelous book called *Multiple Offense and Defenses.*[2] This book became the baseline for my coaching philosophy. I learned to adopt good ideas when I heard them and incorporated them into my teams and personal life as well. I learned to be versatile and teachable.

Being open to new and great ideas is a key foundation for growth as a senior leader. The Father is full of good ideas, and He doles them out freely. We must simply be willing to hear and accept them. He provides fresh ideas in Scripture from the Holy Spirit and from people. We war against jealousy and envy within our members. When one of our friends, coworkers, subordinates, or peers comes up with a good idea, we want our spirits to rejoice and be receptive to learning.

Familiarity is another dangerous adversary we all need to be aware of. "Familiarity breeds contempt"—the truth of this common and well-spoken axiom can destroy our willingness to learn from others. Familiarity also keeps us from acknowledging growth and maturity in others and ourselves. We become unable to learn from the people God has placed around us.

Being teachable and receptive are key ingredients the Father looks for when He is promoting us. Great coaches create an environment that

---

2 Dean Smith, *Multiple Offense and Defenses* (Benjamin Cummings, 1998).

promotes partnership with the team vision. They easily listen to players' and other coaches' input and quickly work with good ideas when they hear them.

Great Coaches Say "We"

Bob Lenz, founder of Life Promotions and keynote speaker to millions of people at conferences worldwide, is a good friend of mine. While distance and assignment keep us apart way too much, we have had great times of close-quarter contact. In 2011 he was touring with the bands Newsboys and Disciple, and I accompanied him for a few days. On the first day I picked him up in Silver Springs, Maryland, at midnight and drove six hours through the night. Bob had graciously agreed to speak at my church in Mexico, New York, the next day.

Driving through the night, we were celebrating and sharing about the goodness of God. During the drive, Bob looked at me and made a statement that was a bit out of context in our discussion. He said, "We never want to be the hero of our own stories."

I went silent, immediately sensing the Holy Spirit was trying to tell me something. It occurred to me that I had given Bob a compact disc of a recent word I had preached. As his words echoed in my ears, I could see I had been glorying in my own brilliance and under-emphasized the feats of others, not to mention Jesus as my source. Meekly smiling, I looked at Bob and said, "You listened to my CD, didn't you?"

Bob is a gentle giant of a man, and through his kindness and gentleness I got to learn from this tremendous man of God about the importance of not being self-absorbed in my own success.

In truth, our successes are never due to our flying solo. Leaders are leaders because people are following them. There is not one leader who does not have a following. Coaches who primarily focus success on their own prowess hold their teams in contempt. A non-verbal message is sent that states, "I can do this without you." What my friend was alerting me to was a tendency to be the hero of my story. Bob reminded me to focus on Jesus and the people He has surrounded me with.

> Without great teams there are no great coaches.

Great coaches say "we" because they know it is the team that makes each success. Each part plays a crucial role in every success.[3] Without great teams there are no great coaches. Our role is to build and raise up the team. Great coaches are intentional in building unity into their approach and team vision.

When we emphasize the role of others, we demonstrate to ourselves, and Jesus, that we can be trusted to acknowledge the people He promotes. We partner with the Father in the promotion of others. There are plenty of examples of the poverty approach of promoting oneself.[4] Our heavenly Father is looking for His remnant to do His work His way, the only way. The Father's way is spoken in the sense of community and family. We become fellow heroes in our collective stories—versus being the heroes of our own stories.

Great Coaches Know the Source of Their Confidence

As we grow in maturity, we learn how to simultaneously marvel in the gifts he has lavished us with and glorify Him for His attributes. Knowing our source means—knowing our source. God wants us to pursue and know Him and His ways. Jeremiah 9:24 says, "'But let him

---

3 1 Corinthians 12

4 Luke 9:46–48

who glories glory in this, that he understands and knows Me, That I am the Lord, exercising lovingkindness, judgment, and righteousness in the earth. For in these I delight,' says the Lord."

Jesus backs this up in John 15:15: "No longer do I call you servants, for a servant does not know what his master is doing, but I have called you friends, for all things that I heard from My Father I have made known to you." It is easy to be caught up in the wonder and glory of God to the point that we feel that the more we know about God the less we know about God, but that is not true. The more we know about God, the more we love Him. We find He is better than we ever knew. It is that increase in knowledge and understanding that we apply to our lives.

I love being overwhelmed by God and never worry about being underwhelmed. He wants to provide all the tools to steward our promotion and needs me to walk in the fullness of who He is to the best of my current understanding.

We do not have time to think about all we lack in Jesus. Prophetic voice Graham Cooke brilliantly states that Jesus works from our present fullness to our future completion. Why should we focus on our lack if He doesn't? It is a good practice for us to go days and weeks without considering our and others' lack. Bill Johnson says he no longer doubts his own motives and does not get caught up in doubting others' motives either. When we place our focus on Jesus, we do not have to worry about false motives or being imprisoned by inevitable illegal thoughts or actions. We know we are not perfect, and so does God, yet we walk blameless while being perfected.

It is critical we understand this about God. Too many people have fallen for a trap that says we are all poor saps just trying to make the best of a tough situation, that God is in control and that all the suffering is somehow in His perfect will. They can quote scriptures that seem to back up this disempowering theology, all taken out of the intended context. False humility states, "I'm worthless and have no good in me. The only good in me is what Jesus does." That simply is not true. We are made in God's image. His DNA is imbedded in us, which means we have His compassion, His kindness, His intensity, His love, all within the spirit man by whom we live. There are many good things about us that are being demonstrated every day as we live our lives in Jesus.

Just because our flesh is at odds with our spirits does not mean we are owned by that flesh. When Paul writes in Romans 7:15, "For what I am doing, I do not understand. For what I will to do, that I do not practice; but what I hate, that I do," he is not talking about a perpetual state but a process we all experience. Jesus does not leave us in that state. Indeed, He delivers us from our "body of death." The absolute truth about Romans 7 is covered in Romans 8:29-30: "For whom He foreknew [us], He also predestined to be conformed to the image of His Son, that He might be the firstborn among many brethren."

Great coaches, and also great leaders, know who they are because they know who their source is, and our source does not leave us in the poverty of our flesh but in the abundance of a life in the Spirit. Armed with that knowledge, great coaches and leaders empower and release their teams into a life in the Spirit.

Chapter 8

Leaders Are Investors

There is a direct correlation between what leaders personally invest in their assignments and what they can rightfully request from partners, teammates, and even heaven. Investing in our assignments is a requirement set by the Lord. Consider Jesus's difficult words in Luke 14:25–35:

> Now great multitudes went with Him. And He turned and said to them, "If anyone comes to Me and does not hate his father and mother, wife and children, brothers and sisters, yes, and his own life also, he cannot be My disciple. And whoever does not bear his cross and come after Me cannot be My disciple. For which of you, intending to build a tower, does not sit down first and count the cost, whether he has enough to finish it—lest, after he has laid the foundation, and is not able to finish, all who see it begin to mock him, saying, 'This man began to build and was not able to finish'? Or what king, going to make war against another king, does not sit down first and consider whether he is able with ten thousand to meet

him who comes against him with twenty thousand? Or else, while the other is still a great way off, he sends a delegation and asks conditions of peace. So likewise, whoever of you does not forsake all that he has cannot be My disciple. "Salt is good; but if the salt has lost its flavor, how shall it be seasoned? It is neither fit for the land nor for the dunghill, but men throw it out. He who has ears to hear, let him hear!"

Our God is an all-in God. It is fascinating that the Greek word for hate is *miseo*. Of all the different forms of love, there is only one form of hate, and Jesus used that word a dozen times. We commonly use this word as hyperbole, but Jesus was making an important point. He was saying to count the cost of discipleship. There is no middle ground. We are talking about the Creator of the universe. Either He is God or He is not.

Jesus was saying, "Trust me. I've got you. I'm going to train you, equip you, empower you, and release you. I know you need rest, and I know you have needs such as shelter and food, praise and empowerment, promotion, satisfaction, and love. Do not put your trust in mother, father, brothers, sisters, others, or yourself. Put it in me."

> Investing in our assignments is a requirement set by the Lord.

It is impossible to fully invest in our assignments if we do not embrace this principle. We will hold back and focus on areas that are a priority in our own thinking. Jesus knew that recipe would not be fulfilling. In essence, our kingdom will compete with His kingdom.

God Is Perfectly Balanced

God fully understands our physical, emotional and spiritual needs. He is a God of body, mind and spirit, and He is perfectly balanced. I know many leaders who struggle with stewarding His promotion when it comes to physical and mental rest. God had need for rest, and so do we.[1] Jesus prioritized rest.[2] Developing a godly balance between work and rest is a most critical component to sustained ministry for ourselves, families, and others. When we rest, we actually give ourselves permission to work hard. Stewarding His promotion requires both. Leaders work harder than anyone else. I have not met a leader yet who accomplished any great thing by going home every night at five o'clock. Leaders need to pray, plan, and prepare before launching each day's work. This investment will require us to steward the full 168 hours we have each week.

The purpose of rest is to rejuvenate our bodies, minds, and spirits, not to perpetuate inactivity. Resting in Him quiets our souls and enhances our environments with peace and joy. It is the mechanism that enables us to recharge our batteries. Laziness, however, is not an attribute God can promote. When we give ourselves large blocks of inactive time, we are out of His balance. I have counseled hundreds of sons and daughters who agonize over their lack of promotion. The two main culprits in their lack of promotion are either hidden sin or laziness. I can spot laziness quickly, because after the third counseling session, I ask them to bring me a full account of the 168 hours in their weeks. Often the lazy ones quit seeking counsel.

Laziness is a deadly disease. Instead of investing our time, we are wasting it. Jesus blatantly called this out and did not pull a punch. Consider Matthew 25:24–30:

---

1 Genesis 2:1–3

2 Mark 6:30–32

Then he who had received the one talent came and said, "Lord, I knew you to be a hard man, reaping where you have not sown, and gathering where you have not scattered seed. And I was afraid, and went and hid your talent in the ground. Look, there you have what is yours."

But his lord answered and said to him, "You wicked and lazy servant, you knew that I reap where I have not sown, and gather where I have not scattered seed. So you ought to have deposited my money with the bankers, and at my coming I would have received back my own with interest. Therefore, take the talent from him, and give it to him who has ten talents.

> Our God is an "all-in" God.

"For to everyone who has, more will be given, and he will have abundance; but from him who does not have, even what he has will be taken away. And cast the unprofitable servant into the outer darkness. There will be weeping and gnashing of teeth."

Note the sin was not in carelessly investing the talent but in hiding the talent. Jesus knew the harvest was plentiful, and laziness, or burying our talents, partners with a demonic attempt to slow or stop the spread of the gospel of the kingdom.[3]

Investing Our 168 Hours

"Time is money" is a commonly used business phrase. While money is used to motivate us to consider the value of time, this saying is completely untrue. Time is a commodity that has infinitely more value

---

3 Luke 10:2

than money.[4] How we invest our time is of great importance to God, and without intentional care, it becomes one of the most undervalued of His gifts to us.

As we are promoted, investing our time with purpose becomes increasingly important.[5] When we are intentional and obedient in allocating our time, the God of five loaves and two fishes helps with multiplication. Mature leaders find great benefit when they apply Psalm 90:12 in practical ways: "So teach us to number our days, that we may gain a heart of wisdom."[6] One practical application that has provided me great return on my time allocation in regard to talent is "numbering my days" on a 168-hour weekly rotation. When we give to or request from someone a slot of that time, we are not able to grant them additional hours in that week in return, so when an impromptu request for four hours comes in, we cannot simply grant a four-hour allocation to total 172 hours for the week. It must come from that 168 hours. The larger the request of our time, the larger the impact is on our week. This is an important concept in developing good habits with how we invest our time. Others' poor planning should not continually become our emergencies.

In my office I have a large whiteboard that blocks off each week's 168 hours. I start every week with a planned accounting for that time. I number my days. In the left-hand column I put my assignments for the week. Then I put columns for each day of the week, and the twenty-four hours of time for each day go in those columns. I invest fifty-six hours per week either asleep or postured before Him and call that time "Rest in Him" time (RIH) on my board. This is one-third of the time each week, so for the remaining 112 hours I need to be very intentional with how I use them.

---

4 Luke 12:13–21

5 Luke 12:49

6 Psalm 90:12

ASSIGNMENTS		M	T	W	T	F	S
REST IN HIM 52½ hrs	12 1 2 3 4	REST IN HIM	REST IN HIM	REST IN HIM	REST IN HIM	REST IN HIM	REST IN HIM
FAMILY & FRIENDS 18 hrs	5 6 7 8 9 10	STUDY FAMILY KTCG	STUDY KTCG	BOOK FAMILY BOOK	KTCG	KTCG	IMAT 3 hrs
KTCG 44½ hrs	11 12 1 2			KTCG ·STAFF MEETING ·MARKETING			BOOK
JOURNEY CENTER 37½	3 4 5	BOARD MEETING Journey University	Journey Center Leaders Meeting	.TFG ·LIST ·OPERATIONS	MEETING W/SEAN		KTC
BOOK 7½ hrs	6 7 8 9			DATE NIGHT W/Robin	KTCG	FAMILY	FAMIL
STUDY 5 hrs	10 11 12	REST IN HIM	REST IN HIM	BOOK REST IN HIM	REST IN HIM	REST IN HIM	REST IN HIM

This design gives me a visual of the impact each request for time has on my assignment. The result is walking by the Spirit with each request. A critical component is keeping Jesus at the front of the decision-making.

Kris Vallotton at Bethel recently blogged,

> If you love God and are passionate about caring for people... if you give people hope and believe in miracles . . . if you pour out your soul for the broken and the poor . . . if you are radically generous . . . you WILL have favor with God and man. BUT if you don't steward the favor of God . . . if you let the fear of man be your shepherd . . . if you convince yourself that you are the savior of the world, obligated to meet every need that you are exposed to . . . YOU WILL CRASH and the crowd will find another savior.[7]

---

7 Kris Vallotton, "Why You Must Manage Your Life," *Krisvallotton.com*, October 26, 2015, http://krisvallotton.com/why-you-must-manage-your-life/

Kris once told me, "David, I have spent the last eighteen years learning how to set boundaries with people." In this blog post he brilliantly articulates an approach we all can learn from and has tapped into the importance of remaining vigilant against time thieves. We should not run a hardnosed, rigid schedule that cannot be deviated from. Jesus very clearly walked with a fluidity of the Spirit and responded to the needs of those around Him. Paul backs that up in Ephesians 5:15–17: "See then that you walk circumspectly, not as fools but as wise, redeeming the time, because the days are evil. Therefore, do not be unwise but understand what the will of the Lord is."

> Time is a commodity that has infinitely more value than money

Lack of intentionality with our time is a demonic strategy used to bait us into time drains that distract from our assignments and drain us physically. Paul wrote about this strategy in Colossians: "Walk in wisdom toward those who are outside, redeeming the time."[8] Note that he does not say, "Do not give time to those who are on the outside, redeeming the time;" rather, he says, "Walk in wisdom toward those who are outside, redeeming the time." Jesus gave us a perfect example of how this works.

> Then Jesus answered and said: "A certain man went down from Jerusalem to Jericho, and fell among thieves, who stripped him of his clothing, wounded him, and departed, leaving him half dead. Now by chance a certain priest came down that road. And when he saw him, he passed by on the other side. Likewise a Levite, when he arrived at the place, came and looked, and passed by on the other side. But a certain Samaritan, as he journeyed, came where he was. And when he saw him, he had compassion. So he went to him and bandaged his wounds, pouring on

---

8 Colossians 4:5

> oil and wine; and he set him on his own animal, brought
> him to an inn, and took care of him. On the next day,
> when he departed, he took out two denarii, gave them to
> the innkeeper, and said to him, 'Take care of him; and
> whatever more you spend, when I come again, I will repay
> you.' So which of these three do you think was neighbor
> to him who fell among the thieves?" And he said, "He who
> showed mercy on him." Then Jesus said to him, "Go and do
> likewise."[9]

Jesus noted the religious people considered themselves too highly to invest their time and resources to help the wounded stranger. Conversely, He celebrated the Samaritan who, stewarding his promotion, showed great compassion and leadership as he invested that which had been granted from the Lord into that wounded man.

Before relocating to our work in the Horseheads/Elmira region of New York, the Lord asked my wife, Robin, and me to sow great resources into the region. In total, we gave nearly $140,000 and countless hours building up the iMatter initiatives and ministering to His kids. At one point I was marveling to a friend of mine that God was providing us an opportunity to give a gift of about $29,000 to help iMatter keep a financial commitment, and my friend callously said, "Brother, I love you, but that is stupid." He seemed angry that I had made the "stupid" investment. What he did not know is that the previous year we gave $50,000 to enable the iMatter festival to happen. I'm glad I didn't tell him that!

I went home dejected and told Robin about the exchange. She just shrugged and said, "It's fine with me if we're stupidly generous." Robin is an amazing woman. She is an actuary by profession but still errs on the side of generosity. In over thirty years of marriage, I have yet to see Robin hesitate in acting generously. I would imagine the priest and

---

9 Luke 10:30–37

the Levite would have thought the Samaritan stupid. What they are missing is the Father's extreme joy at watching His sons and daughters walk in radical generosity. God is the most generous person ever, and that generosity is a trait He transferred to us and much enjoys watching us overflow in.

Extreme generosity demonstrates a level of trust that a poverty mind-set cannot experience. Leaders who easily invest their resources recognize that God's resources are endless and not at risk of running out. It is ironic that we declare our God owns the cattle on a thousand hills,[10] yet our behavior can exhibit a fear of running out of resources.

God's faithfulness is unwavering. He knows our needs and covers them completely.[11] God can sneeze money. The "stupid" donation of $29,000 was the total liquid assets Robin and I could lay our hands on. We had $29,025 in our savings account, most of it earmarked for our daughter's college education. We made the donation on the first Saturday of September 2011. In October 2011, my company was selected to negotiate a deal between a large Timberland Investment Organization and media mogul John Malone, the largest private landowner in the United States. The transaction was for a whopping $298 million. I was paid $108,000 for what added up to be four days of work. I love God's "stupid" math.

---

10 Psalm 50:10

11 Philippians 4:19

Section 3

FOUR LEVELS OF LEADERSHIP

Chapter 9

Leading Without a Title

Have you ever thought about the first time you demonstrated leadership? Take a moment and think back to your earliest days. When was the first time you took a stand on a position, in a relationship, or in defense of another person? Can you go back to when you were eight or nine years old? Perhaps in junior high?

For me, it goes back to my early teens. My parents were foster parents, and in 1968 they adopted African-American twins, a boy and a girl. For us it was normal, and they instantly became part of the family with no distinction from bloodlines, yet in the late 1960s open racism was still very much tolerated. By the time I reached my early teens, I grew an intense hatred of bigotry. Any derogatory word associated with people of color would quickly launch me into physical confrontation. The twins would tell you they saw me come unglued on more than one occasion. They did not need to be present for this to happen. For every fight they were present for, there were five fights they were not.

Taking a stand when we are young can be our first moments in stepping out in leadership. It will not be perfect, and we may not even be on the right side, but when we demonstrate a willingness not to follow the crowd, to stand up to an injustice, to stop someone from being bullied, or to speak up for righteousness when others are misbehaving, we are walking out the God-given leadership mantle He has imbedded in our DNA.

Taking a stand when we are young can be our first moments in stepping out in leadership.

From our early days, God is preparing us to lead. Each life is sprinkled with opportunities to demonstrate a willingness to follow our Holy Spirit-led consciences, even to the detriment of our own comfort. Scripture recounts the development of sons and daughters before they held a title. Abram and Sarah's early barrenness,[1] Joseph's interactions with his brothers,[2] Moses in the land of Midian,[3] Ruth serving Naomi,[4] David serving his family,[5] Esther providing early wisdom,[6] Daniel and his teenage friends,[7] Jesus in the temple at twelve,[8] and young men named John Mark and Silas.[9]

Each biblical story recounts opportunities similar to those we are presented with in our own journeys. The adversary would whisper that Bible characters are anomalies, individuals set aside for a great purpose that is unique among men, yet Jesus counters that lie throughout His life. From His first documented teaching in Matthew 5-7 to His last teaching in John 14-17, Jesus presents to us our leadership mantle and His promotional heart. Training begins at an early age.

---

1 Genesis 11:30

2 Genesis 37:4

3 Exodus 2:11

4 Ruth 1:16

5 1 Samuel 1:11

6 Esther 2:10

7 Daniel 4

8 Luke 2:42

9 Acts 15:38

Changing the Environment

Opportunities to lead without a title are presented to us daily. Even the most senior officials with the most distinguished titles are not recognized everywhere. Regardless of position, when leaders walk into the grocery store, they are just other shoppers. As believers, we are intentionally placed into the world to be the light. From the start of the day with our families and through every moment in a public setting, we have the grand assignment to carry the atmosphere of heaven with us.

Each time we are in a setting where the people around us do not know our position or title, we have a unique opportunity to shine light where there is darkness uninhibited by any agenda that would otherwise accompany our position. As unattached strangers, we can change the world with simple acts of kindness.

> We are intentionally placed in the world to be the light.

Satan would have our culture separate and self-absorbed. His primary goal is to get us into his lonely world. He loves to separate us, to get us to ignore each other, to pass each other by without recognition or acknowledgment. It was intentional that Satan waited until Jesus was alone and physically weak to attack Him in the desert.

Jesus was totally in tune with His surroundings. He was a fervent study of people's posture, behavior, and actions. Jesus acknowledged the people around Him whom others rejected, and He trained and equipped, then empowered and released His disciples to do the same.[10] God desires a bride who promotes a culture of unity and self-awareness, of identity. His intention is that we lead in every circumstance, that we would be the salt, the light, the city. Jesus knows that we, as sons and

---

10   Luke 10:1

daughters, carry the greatest title ever given. We can and should lead without further need of position.

Every day is loaded with opportunities to change an atmosphere of hopelessness to one of hope and purpose. In every store, every intersection, every workplace, and every center of activity are sons and daughters of the Most High God waiting to be revealed.[11]

Our Internal Atmosphere

Before we can lead others, we need to learn to lead ourselves. It is the only place to start. Learning to lead without a title is a joyous and fabulous process culminated by the moment we realize our identities are not connected to man's recognition.[12] We learn to feed our own spirit man through posture,[13] study,[14] personal worship,[15] and abiding in Him.[16]

The atmosphere we carry internally is the atmosphere we will create externally. If our internal view of self is negative, our internal atmosphere will be negative, but if our internal view of self is as son or daughter, co-heir, friend of Jesus, our internal atmosphere will be heaven here on earth.

> The atmosphere we carry internally is the atmosphere we will create externally.

---

11 Romans 8:19

12 Galatians 1:10

13 Romans 12:1–2

14 2 Timothy 2:15

15 Psalm 103:1

16 John 15:7

We need to develop a culture of honor, acknowledgment, and promotion within our own lives. Danny Silk's book *Culture of Honor*[17] is a brilliant read on this topic. We work within our strengths and bravely admit and overcome our weaknesses. We develop a lifestyle of building upon incremental successes and overcoming mistakes. Many people consider mistakes as failures, but nothing could be farther from the truth.

If success is the building block of our leadership resume, learning from our mistakes is the concrete foundation of that building block. Mistakes are ideal training tools. They are made both innocently through neglect and intentionally through tolerated weakness. Each mistake is an opportunity to discover what is not working within our lives.

Developing our positive internal atmosphere puts us at ease with the learning process. We view correction as God's way of protecting us and those around us.[18] Because we recognize that we are not in competition, we can learn from others without being threatened by their input. There is a contagious peace that comes with a positive internal heart posture. We are the calm in the storm, slow with our opinions, and we listen before we talk. We walk with an air of authority that is not intimidating but evident of the jurisdictional transfer of authority from Jesus to us as co-heirs, at one with the Godhead.

Spirit of Adoption

If we were to walk into most churches in America, we would note the dynamic of the spirit of adoption at work. There will be people who are up front, those who are in the middle, the transition zone, and those who remain in the shadows. While this dynamic is in part an inevitable lifecycle as people become accustomed to their surroundings, it is sad

---

17 Danny Silk, *Culture of Honor: Sustaining a Supernatural Environment* (Shippensburg, Pa.: Destiny Image Publishers, Inc., 2009).

18 Hebrews 12:6

that many hang in the transition zone or the shadows for their entire lives. Fear or lack of hope keeps them from seeking more, and they are lulled into a life of complacency. It is as though they are orphans, not yet living as adopted sons and daughters.

The longer orphans live without adequate affirmation and a developed purpose in Jesus, the more likely they are to seek affirmation in the wrong places. Unfulfilled, these precious sons and daughters withdraw from deep relationships, interacting with others only with narrowly defined, self-established guidelines. Ultimately, these wonderful people reside in the shadows. Withdrawn and untrusting, they remain wounded and afraid of relationship. We have an amazing and continual opportunity to partner with the Holy Spirit to give the withdrawn and untrusting people an expresso shot to their internal atmospheres. We welcome them into the family as adopted sons or daughters, as we once were welcomed as well.

Paul illustrates our position in Romans 8:14–19:

> For as many as are led by the Spirit of God, these are sons of God. For you did not receive the spirit of bondage again to fear, but you received the Spirit of adoption by whom we cry out, "Abba, Father." The Spirit Himself bears witness with our spirit that we are children of God, and if children, then heirs—heirs of God and joint heirs with Christ, if indeed we suffer with Him, that we may also be glorified together.
>
> For I consider that the sufferings of this present time are not worthy to be compared with the glory which shall be revealed in us. For the earnest expectation of the creation eagerly waits for the revealing of the sons of God.

Godly leaders recognize that not only have they received the "Spirit of adoption by whom we cry out, 'Abba, Father,'"[19] but each person has, imbedded in his or her core, a hunger to be adopted.

We should not be surprised when orphans act like orphans. Instead, we should walk in tune to the Holy Spirit and be on-demand to connect orphans to the family. Read the following letter from the heart of someone who attended our iMatter festival this year.

> Dear iMatter,
>
> I really wanted to say thank you. I was at the festival, and I had a great time. I am not religious at all . . . but with that said, one person did really open up my mind a bit. I don't recall his name, but he had a white hat, Dan I think. I was in a bad way, and he saw that. I feel real bad because when he said Jesus loves me, I spit in his face. That man didn't get mad; he just told me again Jesus loves me! He started to cry. That man saved my mind, and I didn't follow through with ending it all. I don't know if you know it but that man touched all my friends.
>
> — I MATTER

At iMatter this story has been repeated hundreds of times. We reach out to orphans, many of whom are considering suicide. Leaders do not need titles to lead; they need the heart of a father. Notice that this young person ended this hand-written note with "I MATTER." Godly leaders carrying Jesus lead with the understanding that each son and daughter matters. We never know when God is going to use us in some obscure but dramatic way to intervene on His behalf to connect an orphan with his or her dad. Godly leaders must stay postured and responsive to the Holy Spirit's nudges. This kind of leadership starts

---

19 Romans 5:18

in the family. As parents, my wife, Robin, and I had only three rules for our daughters. Rule one: Seek out your identity in God. Rule two: Treat all people well. Rule three: Do your best in school. In short, we taught our daughters to lead at an early age. We taught them not to be influenced in areas of poor behavior but to influence those around them to their best understanding of godly behavior.

Of course, this requires Robin and me to live these rules out as well. Our families have front-row seats to our leadership, and the same rules apply to us. Our children will not follow us as they grow into adults if we lead without godly character. Even if we follow rules two and three, without a developed God-given identity, our children are left to a faith dependent on Mom and Dad instead of having their own vibrant and growing relationships with the Godhead.

Robin and I may never get "Parent of the Year" awards, as our daughters have been relatively easy and compliant children, yet we are still asked, "What parenting skills did you apply to have your daughters so in love with Jesus?" It is a legit question. Our twenty-five-year-old is an "all-in" lover and servant of the Father, Jesus, and the Holy Spirit. She is a brilliant worshiper and prophetic daughter. Our nine-year-old was given the gift of tongues at seven years old. She has been overwhelmed by the Holy Spirit and has visually seen God in worship. The only answer we can give to that question is we are as intentional in placing them in His presence as we are at placing ourselves in His presence, and we teach them how to feed themselves spiritually.

Our family has as a high-core value experiencing His manifest presence as a family and are intentional about making His presence welcome and evident in our home. We are careful about what movies we watch and in what tone and language we communicate. We look for opportunities where the corporate body is in a unity of worship and adoration and attend these functions as a family. Sometimes it is in our home church, and sometimes it is in a conference setting such as Global Awakening's Voice of the Prophets or Voice of the Apostles. At such events our daughters have been influenced by tremendous and relevant voices in our culture.

Jamie and Emily Galloway are just the voices we want speaking into our daughters' lives. They are prophetic culture-shapers for the kingdom and have become close friends with our family. Robin and I have deep gratitude for them that began when Jamie ministered to our eldest daughter, Cassia, at a Voice of the Prophets conference. His timely and relevant words were just what Cassia needed at a sensitive time in her life.

Godly leaders understand that how we lead our family is how we will lead others.[20] So many times moral failures could have been circumvented by understanding and responding to the symptoms showing up in the privacy of our homes. A developed culture of God's presence in our hearts and our homes is the blueprint for the developed culture of His presence outside our homes.

---

20   1 Timothy 3:4–5

Chapter 10

Leading Subordinates

Leadership training begins without our even knowing it. It starts the very first time we are given a level of authority over another person, perhaps as an older brother or sister, a babysitter, the captain of a sports team, or the team lead on a school project. Commonly these experiences are much like being thrown into the deep end of the pool and told to swim. We may receive a few guidelines and a "Let me know if you need anything," but then it's "splash, splash."

Most of us could write many chapters on how not to lead. Through my teenage years my leadership gift was not apparent. No one asked me to babysit or lead a scout troop or class project. When I was assigned to watch my siblings, it was not pretty. I fed myself from the fat and clothed myself with the wool, as referred to in Ezekiel 34. I raided the refrigerator, monopolized the television, and made sure everyone knew I was in charge.

I was fired from all my first jobs. I worked on a farm and was fired for being reckless on a tractor. I worked for my dad's company and was fired for sloppy work. I got a job at the local ice cream shop, made my friends huge ice cream cones, and put beer in a milkshake container to drink while working. I also punched a guy through the ice cream window for repeatedly ringing the buzzer for service. Yep, I was fired.

Out of job options, I joined the United States Army. For the first time in my life, I would be trained and equipped to lead. It was there I first learned how to embrace authority. I learned that agreement was not a requirement of unity. I learned success was more likely if we worked as a team. I learned how to rely on others and how to be relied upon. I learned that even in a structure where rank should insure compliance, it was still a volunteer army. Leaders still needed a developed set of skills in motivating people, resolving conflict, articulating vision, and maintaining healthy boundaries.

Leading Free People

> The human race has the
> freedom to choose how to
> act and react.

When God created us, He set in motion a physical law that would remain constant throughout the ages. Regardless of circumstances or governing bodies, the human race has the freedom to choose how to act and react. From Adam and Eve in the Garden through the end of the millennium, God gives us the choice. The truth spoken by Joshua remains a constant reminder of that choice:

> And if it seems evil to you to serve the Lord, choose for yourselves this day whom you will serve, whether the gods which your fathers served that were on the other side of the River, or the gods of the Amorites, in whose land you dwell. But as for me and my house, we will serve the Lord.[1]

---

1 Joshua 24:15

The United States is the world's leading example of freedom for its people. We are founded on a basic principle that all mankind is created equal and provided inalienable rights. According to Merriam-Webster, inalienable means "unable to be taken away from or given away by the possessor."[2]

In America we have something President Herbert Hoover called "rugged individualism." The concept was that each person was ultimately responsible for himself or herself. Over time, this phrase has grown into a fiercely independent spirit that permeates much of our environment. We learn that at a certain age we can fly the coop, split the scene, leave the nest, and there is nothing our parents or guardians can legally do to prevent it. We can be the master of our own destiny, captain of our own ship, the decision-maker in our lives. Rugged individualism is so strongly part of the American fabric that many people feel no call to serve under the authority of anyone else without being paid or forced to do so by laws.

For so many people, a lack of appropriate fathering has ensured a fiercely independent approach to life. Daily dependence on the Godhead is undeveloped, and this spirit of rugged individualism can transcend any concept of being in and under authority. Given this paradigm, it is truly providential we have not self-destructed, but through grace, mercy, and His wisdom, we can learn to lead in an environment that despises authority. Godly leaders realize that any approach of "Just do what you are told" will be an unsuccessful model. We will eventually find that our Father himself has granted a freedom we are not to take away.

Jesus's model works much better. His model was not one of issuing orders but one of training and equipping, then empowering and releasing. He spent significant time with His Father and trained himself to listen well. Jesus's prophetic gifting was well developed, and He would commonly

---

2 "inalienable," Merriam-Webster. https://www.merriam-webster.com/dictionary/inalienable

preempt problems by knowing what people were thinking.[3] Leaders need to develop and walk daily in a prophetic gifting. We encourage, exalt, and comfort the people we are leading. We walk in wisdom, words of knowledge, and revelation. Part of training and equipping is teaching the benefit of raw obedience. Obedience does not mean turning off the brain. Leaders do not want robots. Mature leaders are able to train their staff and their teams that complying to instruction is part of maturity and will equip them to utilize their unique gift sets.

You're Fired!

I admit to enjoying the first few seasons of Donald Trump's *Apprentice* show,[4] perhaps because I have been fired so many times; however, being released from a job is not always bad. Back in the early 90s, I was working for a construction company owned by two elders at our church. I was able to do the work but had no passion for it. I was young, and the lack of passion was noticed in a variety of ways: missing timelines, showing up late for work, grumpiness, and no commitment to excellence being among them.

The owners and I had relationship outside of work, and I was like a little brother to one of them. They kept me on but with a watchful eye. Always encouraging me to embrace the opportunities given to me, they soon realized that change was needed. Finally, one of the owners called me into his office. He said, "Dave, I really like you, and so does everyone here. We really enjoy your humor and personality, but it's evident to my partner and I that you're not happy here. We don't want to fire you, but we think you should find another job. This is not who you are designed to be." They gave me my last two weeks of pay as a severance gift, and I was let go.

---

3 Matthew 12:25; 22:16; Mark 2:8; Luke 6:8; John 2:25

4 Mark Burnett, *The Apprentice*, Television, National Broadcasting Company, January 2008

That act of kindness was initially painful, but it served as a catalyst, launching me into a career path and producing millions of dollars in income for the King family. Conflict resolution is a necessary component of leading subordinates; handling conflict in all its forms is an act of kindness. Jesus had a wonderful blend of patience for others and a willingness to address their behaviors that would eventually lead to pain for someone and the people around them. He brought correction kindly and directly.

Leaders need to study how Jesus brought correction to others and look beyond the surface. From His discussion with the rich young ruler[5] to His defense of the prostitute;[6] from Nicodemus[7] to James's and John's mothers request,[8] Jesus could rebuke without rejecting. He brought gentle but firm correction. He avoided unproductive conflict[9] yet was willing to show great passion in defending righteousness and holiness.[10] He allowed dissenters to leave.

It is not possible, practical, or kind to avoid conflict at all costs. Small infractions of judgment can develop into continued poor behavior and are important areas for leaders to address. Unnecessary avoidance ensures the volume level of the inevitable confrontation will increase. The volume is not related to simply loud shouting. In truth, yelling demonstrates lack of self-control and sacrifices authority. Volume most frequently shows up in the intensity of a situation. Important issues should be addressed by a simple word of correction, because when left to grow, they can turn into failures in completing tasks, in addition to moral failures and relational strains.

---

5   Mark 10:21

6   John 8:11

7   John 3:10

8   Matthew 20:22

9   Luke 4:28–30

10   Matthew 23

The longer repeated problems go unaddressed, the greater the chance the issues will be complicated by other factors. Our adversary goes to and fro throughout the earth looking for conflict in which he can weasel in and multiply its impact. As godly leaders, we have the obligation to address character issues within our staff and teams as a preventative measure to ensure that they do not magnify.

Collectively, we can foil the works of the enemy and build godly authority and behavior into our community, even knowing it will not be perfect. People may revert back to independence. A gentle but firm approach will be reproach to the independent spirit.[11]

Vision Is Not a Secret

Jesus was intentional and strategic when imparting knowledge, understanding, and wisdom into His team. He walked in perfect wisdom, knowing when and how to do it. Jesus never kept secrets but was sensitive to how much information we can handle. Consider John 16:12: "I still have many things to say to you, but you cannot bear them now," which was spoken in the sermon of John 14–17.

> Jesus never kept secrets but was sensitive to how much we can handle.

This is truly mind-boggling. Jesus makes that statement at the same time He provided the information in John 17, that we are now one with the Godhead. He could do this because He knew the Holy Spirit would provide the training on how to apply it. There is a truism in business that states, "Information is power," and Jesus knew it too well. Jesus knew the higher truth is, it is how people handle information that establishes the power, through His granted authority.

---

11 Proverbs 15:32

We honor people by keeping them informed early in the process with all the pertinent information "they can bear." Jesus gave us full disclosure to the extent we were ready. Just as Philippians 2:3 reminds us to "let nothing be done through selfish ambition or conceit, but in lowliness of mind let each esteem others better than himself," Jesus did not withhold information to maintain His lofty position. He intentionally gave us the inside scoop to empower us to join Him in that position.

Jesus wanted His disciples to carry God's kingdom so they could advance it. Therefore, He preached the kingdom from His first sermon to the day He was taken up. It is not possible for our teams or staff to carry a vision they do not hear about or understand. This can take time and a commitment to repeat over and over. We are in the tenth year at iMatter, and our national growth is due to the maturity of people who understand and carry the iMatter vision. We still keep vision-related topics and stories at the forefront of our meetings and events.

It is imperative to keep the vision in front of the team. Otherwise, we forget why we are doing what we are doing. It is the *why* that drives the *what*. When our *why* gets skewed, eventually the *what* will get skewed. Keeping teams and staff informed ensures a cooperative team spirit and a welcoming atmosphere to new ideas and improvements in carrying out the team vision.

Maintain Team Health

Appropriately leading subordinates requires a balance of honor, acknowledgment, and promotion. We always keep in mind that we are leading sons and daughters of the Most High God, and He is a jealous parent. It is also the way to counter the independent spirit. We focus on little successes and recognition of growth. When necessary, course correction is done with ample notice and should not be surprising to the people receiving correction. Never give people tests they do not know they are taking. We promote through acknowledgment that God has first promoted, and our role is to partner with what God has established. We then train and equip, not lord over.[12]

As we travel from glory to glory,[13] all sons and daughters are in the process of being refined and promoted. Whether as parents, supervisors at work, or in positions at church, all our authority is designed to mimic Jesus's authority. "For who is greater, he who sits at the table, or he who serves? Is it not he who sits at the table? Yet I am among you as one who serves."[14]

Although Jesus issued instructions to His followers that He expected to be followed, He never left His place as servant leader, right up to His death on the cross. The more authority we carry, the less we need to issue orders. Paul was on to something when he wrote, "Imitate me, just as I also imitate Christ."[15] Paul recognized he had to issue fewer demands and requirements on his followers as he himself followed Jesus's example. He developed within his staff and teams a unity of the Spirit that made his instructions and requests easy to follow.

The more authority we carry,
the less we need to issue orders.

---

12   1 Peter 5:3

13   2 Corinthians 3:16–18

14   Luke 22:27

15   1 Corinthians 11:1

Chapter 11

Leading Veterans

At seventeen years of age, Joseph walked in the promotional favor of his father. However, he was tested by how he honored those with more age and experience than him. Wisdom suggests a low heart posture that recognizes an assignment Joseph had no way of being ready for. Hence, he needed to draw on the experience and support of his older brothers. In his immaturity, Joseph became overwhelmed with his mantle and chose haughtiness and bragged his way into a pit.[1]

In Joseph's haste to obtain what the Lord had intended for him, he prematurely tried to assume his position. This created all kinds of pitfalls—pun intended. Instead of seeking relationship with his elder brothers, Joseph's actions produced separation. His lack of humility, even considering the ill-conceived way Jacob had shown favoritism toward him, was evidenced by his brothers' hatred of him. Likewise, when we prematurely assume more than what is being offered, we set up a chain of events that shows our immaturity more than our capabilities. We suggest to others that we are arrogant enough to think

---

1 Genesis 37:1–24

we already have the tools we need instead of patiently acquiring the skills to grow into a position.

Instead of wearing the special tunic his father had given him, what if Joseph had gracefully found a way to redirect this favoritism to his elder brothers? What if he had quietly pondered what God was speaking to him through the dreams instead of gloating first to his brothers, then his father and mother? Was the pit part of God's perfect plan or a consequence of pride and haughtiness?

Haughtiness says, "I have a title over you;" humility says, "I need your council and partnership to be successful." Haughtiness says, "I need to prove to you I am in charge;" humility says, "I need to earn your respect." Haughtiness says, "I'm too busy and important to acknowledge your experience;" humility says, "I honor the sacrifices and wisdom you carry."

As we are promoted in the kingdom, perhaps we will be promoted into positions that place us in authority over those who are older and have more experience. Through these positions, we will have opportunities to take the same tests Joseph took. Joseph was never promoted to the position of being older than his more seasoned brothers. His promotion in the kingdom did not circumvent the honor he was required to give Jacob and Rachel and his elder brothers. This dynamic is one I have seen repeated many times over and indeed I have fallen victim to as well. Only when we have learned enough to pass this test are we truly positioned to carry more senior positions in the kingdom.

Maintaining Honor

When afforded the opportunities to lead veterans and those older than us, we need to develop a deep commitment to maintaining a position of honor and respect. That will not always be easy. Our promotion can be especially challenging to the veterans around us who have their own aspirations. They may view our promotion as their demotion. How many of Joseph's elder brothers secretly wanted that tunic? As our assignment always includes partnering with the Holy Spirit to affirm others, we will be wonderfully positioned to affirm those seniors around us who hunger for more and are willing to be released into their own promotion.

Maintaining respect for our elders does not mean we should be unnecessarily held back by jealousy or envy. For example, Jesse's youngest son, David, walked in a tremendous and uncommon relationship with God. He walked in the mantle before it was made public. David's courage and faith afforded him great victories in the quiet places, and when God promoted David, his eldest brother, Eliab, could not see it.[2] It is noteworthy that Eliab had been present when Samuel first anointed David. A closer look shows that God had noticed something in Eliab's heart that He found objectionable. It is clear Eliab held an objection to being overlooked, a heart posture we all can relate to until we recognize that God is the Author of our promotion. Undeterred from walking in the mantle of a king, David slew Goliath and proceeded to fulfill all God had promised him.

When we approach veterans of the faith with honor and respect, we prove the Father right in His selection of us for the promotion. It is a refusal to an illegal competitive spirit, a statement to the atmosphere that we find glory not in our own abilities but only in understanding of the Father's purposes.[3] Satan makes it easy for us to get caught up in the jealousy of other people's promotions. We will have plenty of opportunities to feel the rejection of those who lack the vision for our position. It is an age-old drama acted out by Cain and Abel, Joseph and his older brothers, David and Eliab, even the prodigal son and his older brother. It is a drama Jesus knew all too well. Nearly every church

---

2   1 Samuel 17:28

3   Jeremiah 9:24

leader, the Pharisees, Sadducees, elders, and teachers of the Law, was adversarial to Jesus.

A surface look shows Jesus confronting these leaders, but we need to go deeper. Jesus's tough words were spoken as a shepherd protecting the flock from a demonic religious spirit. He spoke specifically to the leaders who were directly under the influence of Satan,[4] who had an intent to mislead the flock. In a short time it became evident that Jesus had been effective in starting a loving process that would bring many of the church leaders into the kingdom.[5]

After Jesus's resurrection, many leaders fully converted,[6] most notably Saul of Tarsus, a Pharisee, and Crispus, the ruler of the synagogue. Jesus won over these veterans of the Jewish faith with the same recipe He won us over with, by His words and His deeds.[7] Jesus's respect for the Pharisee Nicodemus is beautiful. He gently guided Nicodemus through the purposes of God. It was Nicodemus who first heard the words of John 3:16-17: "For God so loved the world that He gave His only begotten Son, that whoever believes in Him should not perish but have everlasting life. For God did not send His Son into the world to condemn the world but that the world through Him might be saved."

Jesus gave great honor to those senior to Him. "Then He spoke to the multitudes and to His disciples, saying, 'The scribes and the Pharisees sit in Moses' seat. Therefore whatever they tell you to observe, that observe and do, but do not do according to their works; for they say, and do not do.'"[8] Jesus knew God had appointed them and positioned them. He knew they had been tested through the fire throughout the

---

4 John 8:44

5 John 12:42

6 Acts 6:7

7 John 14:11

8 Matthew 23:1–3

longevity of their lives. Though Jesus was critical of some of their ways, He still honored their God-appointed placement.

As godly leaders, we have the same responsibility to honor veterans and those older to us. Veterans have the benefit of time and experience that adds tremendous capacity to our teams and staff. Experience is a fine tuner. As I get older, I love surrounding myself with youthful exuberance because of the lack of inhibition and simple faith. It is wonderful to behold and partner with. Though they are at times reckless, when properly channeled, that recklessness will accomplish tasks that veterans might not even try. However, if I had only younger staff and teams, they would run me into the ground. Honest veterans admire youthful exuberance and will never attempt to inhibit boldness, preferring instead to help shape the approach to improve success.

Because they have gone through countless risk and reward scenarios, veterans provide important guidance. Veterans have a balance that is needed for endurance and a sagacity that will avoid unnecessary loss. They know where the enemy likes to set his snares. These are areas that demonstrate lack of godly character and can entrap us, areas such as hidden bitterness, unclean thoughts or behaviors, or prideful speech. Snares are best set in our predictable path of travel, and our senior advisors are vigilant to assist leaders in avoiding them when possible.

At Journey Center we have a wonderful team of veterans. They know how to father and mother when needed or be a big brother and sister when needed. It is wonderful to watch these fifty-to-seventy-year-old counselors who are free from feeling that they are in competition with those they are serving. This freedom is an important part of the selection process. Veterans who understand how to lead and know that God owns our promotion are invaluable. Free from being in competition with their authority figures, these senior leaders provide stability and timely words of encouragement along with their honed abilities in performing tasks.

Conversely, an unholy spirit of competition is what disqualified many of the church leaders in the New Testament. It is why Jesus said to heed their words but to not follow their deeds. Disgruntled veterans adversely affect teams and staff when they are left unchallenged. By their seniority, they have a natural position of visual leadership. Their acts of disunity will be noticed even if their words are correct. This is precisely what Jesus was calling out in Matthew 23. The scribes wrote what they were supposed to write, and the Pharisees taught what they were supposed to teach, but neither group acted appropriately.

Great coaches allow increased levels of freedom of movement and decisions by senior staff within the confines of the team or corporate vision. Although energy levels may decline, motivation levels should not. At fifty-three, I am finding a fifteen-minute afternoon nap advantageous. I find I do not have the physical capacity I had through my forties, yet I cannot let this lack of energy reduce motivation or excitement for the tasks God has given me. This has required me to be selective with what I say yes to.

As we build our teams, we need to allow our senior staff the flexibility to manage their stamina. This is not unlike Kobe Bryant's last years with the LA Lakers. While Bryant's timeliness and presence at practices was required, his output at the heavy practice sessions was reduced, and his playing time in the games was reduced to maximize his effectiveness at what he was really good at: scoring. The amount of exertion was Bryant's call, but he still obeyed team rules, attended team meetings, gave crucial perspective when called on, helped coaches negotiate the minefield, and never undermined his coaches. There are few sports championships won by all young teams or all veteran teams. The best opportunity for successful teams is a blend of both youthful exuberance and veteran experience. Appropriately leading veterans will allow us to feed into them and to be fed by them.

It is wonderful being led by a younger leader. One of my spiritual sons is Jake Luhrs, the lead singer of the Grammy-nominated metal core band

August Burns Red. Jake and I have developed a deep relationship based on love, mutual respect, and common assignment. As a counselor, I consider myself on Jake's team. Although I am twenty years older and a mentor to him, in many ways I serve him.

Jake is wise enough to seek wisdom for his life and draw from experience and sagacity that comes from age, but he also gives back in tremendous ways. Recently he visited me for a few days, and on our drive back to his home in Lancaster, Pennsylvania, he asked me a probing question that uncovered a wound I had been carrying for twenty-five years. Gently and with the authority he carries as one of God's sons and a friend of Jesus, Jake walked me through deliverance from this wound.

For you veterans reading this chapter, please hear this: We are not in competition with our sons or those younger than us. It is a reality to God's heart of promotion that we can be promoted to a place of serving our sons. We partner with the Father's heart when we allow ourselves to be part of a team led by someone younger and less mature.

Chapter 12

Leading Our Leaders

I love speaking on the topic of leadership. There are many misconceptions and misguided concepts that bypass simple truth. One of my favorite topics to speak about is leading those in authority over us. The topic itself is sure to draw attention from both sides of the authority realm, those in authority and those under authority. Many people in authority do not recognize the joy of being led by those we have under our leadership and many under authority do not recognize the joy of leading their covering.

Peter could have written volumes on how not to lead those in authority over us, although he did write two books on how to lead properly. While he was with Jesus, he frequently offered his unsolicited opinions to Him. Peter's willingness to put it out there brought responses from Jesus that appeared at times harsh. However, Jesus never corrected Peter's forthrightness; He only challenged his rashness or lack of faith.

Peter seemed to have an inherent knowledge that he was born to lead, a trait many of the most successful young leaders of today carry. He offered Jesus his perspective, ideas, bold moves, and even correction. Peter was the only one to get out of the boat; he was the one who proclaimed Jesus as the Messiah; he was the one to draw his sword in the garden. When Peter's strength failed him, he wept bitterly, went into his cave, and came out stronger. Ultimately, Peter's leadership was recognized, and the promotion that followed was chronicled as the base command for leadership for the rest of time.

At Journey Center we have a great group of young people who carry the Peter anointing. There is no end to perspectives, ideas, bold moves, and deep love of the Father. These younger sons and daughters frequently lead us to the altar, to the microphone to pray, to raise hands and be humble before God. I watch and marvel at this chosen generation leading us in the race to the throne room. They seem to more easily embrace the concept that abiding is a residency and not a temporary stop than many who are older in the Lord.

There is great joy to be experienced when we lead the people in authority over us. It releases something inside that says we are here not only to receive but to give back as well. The mentor's role is to train, equip, empower, and release. The protégé's role is to learn and give back. It is impossible to release a younger son or daughter who refuses the promotion. We can train only those who will be trained, equip only those willing to be equipped, empower only those who will be empowered, and release only those who will accept the mantle. It is through relationship that these things happen.

> The protégé's role is to learn and give back.

Peter's willingness to lead while being trained made him a candidate for his promotion. He even tried to train Jesus,[1] yet it was his submissive heart that provided the fuel to the fire of his boldness. There is no better way to teach walking under authority than by walking under authority ourselves. All the while Peter was figuring out his authority, he served Jesus, who provided spiritual, physical, and emotional covering. It is

---

1 Matthew 16:22

easy to adopt a philosophy that considers relationship with our covering one-sided, that it is always up to our fathers and mothers to feed into us, even though Peter, James, and John fed back into Jesus.

I have had countless young men and women ask to become my spiritual sons and daughters. A son or daughter's ability to feed back into a father is the determining factor of a relationship that will either endure or be only a temporary relationship. Both can be productive; however, many of these men and women are really looking for affirmation. I note that as soon as affirmation turns to correction, they disappear. It is a harsh reality of leadership. Many people simply do not understand that their leaders are human, with human emotions and human needs that also need affirmation.

By sowing into our leaders, we create a symbiotic relationship versus a parasitic one. It opens the communication both ways. It allows our leaders to see how a person in authority can learn and discover new heights through those they lead. People who submit themselves to their godly authority and spend time feeding into their bodies, souls, and spirits are certain to be fully enriched by the relationship and most likely will remain connected for a long time.

> By sowing into our leaders, we create a symbiotic relationship versus a parasitic one.

Leading people in authority over us requires an understanding of our identities and an established confidence to speak truth when the opportunity is presented. Fear can inhibit us from providing insights our leaders may not have. If we live concerned about man's promotion or demotion, we will be tempted to speak what we believe our leaders want to hear versus what is truth.

One of my most cherished spiritual daughters is Alden Anderson. Alden is one of those young 20-somethings whom you would hire for every job. She is detail-oriented, works with organized lists, and is very thorough. Alden has the Peter edge. She has been one of our team leaders with iMatter from the earliest days of the foundation, yet these traits are not what makes her so valuable to us at iMatter. We have hundreds of volunteers come through this outreach, many of them very talented. What separates Alden from so many of her contemporaries is her forthright approach to problem-solving. For the first four years of our working together, Alden and I were bound to have an incident that would result in an emotional discussion.

In our eight years of working together at iMatter, and now other initiatives, Alden has never rebuffed my words of correction. Even when she did not agree, she would state her case, accept any instruction, and go about the business of completing her mission. Like Peter, she does not have a passive-aggressive bone in her body. Passive-aggressive behavior has no role in the kingdom, or anywhere else for that matter. Passive-aggressive behavior is a saboteur. It is a demonic initiative that attempts to undermine ultimate success. It says, "Because I disagree with my leader, I'm not going to fully support the initiative," but agreement is not required for unity.

Success is based not on full agreement about what offenses or defenses teams should run, but the commitment of the team to accomplish what plays are called. Though there may be frequent disagreement among coaches and players in the play that is called, once it is called, each coach and player commits to the ultimate success. The reality of unity is that even when a poor play is called, success is possible through total commitment to the play. Total commitment is an important trait to carry through life. As subordinates, we are positioned to lead our covering even when in disagreement with decisions by committing to their execution and success.

It is not possible to lead those in authority over us if we have a sense of *coup de tat* in our spirits. Through most of my coaching career I was the head assistant coach. Through grace I recognized early in my career that if a head coach thought I was after his job or looking to illegally gain position with a team by undermining him, he would not be comfortable granting me authority he might otherwise prefer. I wish I could state this came from a biblical perspective in those early days, but it was likely due to my time in the army. God gifted me with an ease of walking under authority. Hence, I did not threaten my superiors.

The "I could do this better" sound bite Satan plays in our minds is dangerous and illegal. It is counter to what wisdom would counsel. Wisdom provides subordinates with a great opportunity to make helpful suggestions and even the freedom to provide a broader, think-tank commentary. Wisdom can be working on the fringes of a particular topic. It is relegated not to the final product but to the process in which we arrive at our destination. Our superiors will be much freer to listen to counsel and open dialog if they do not have to sort through an illegal agenda that whispers "Overthrow." This is most evidenced when conversations turn to frequent disagreements with superiors over an extended period of time. This unhealthy environment causes stress and lack of peace. Prolonged, it becomes a front-page item and saps energy from the team. Overthrow says, "This leader should step down," where unity says, "I should come into alignment."

There are times we are directed differently in life than where our leaders are headed. The question will always come down to "What does Jesus want?" I have had an environment become untenable when Jesus was saying it was time for Robin and me to change our environment. These changes should always be done peacefully and under covering.

I felt we should move to Elmira, New York, two years before Robin did. I received my preparation orders from the Holy Spirit in 2010. However, Robin was not ready, and until she was, we were not released. Through the next two years it became evident our assignment could not be accomplished at our old church. I was a senior elder in the house, frequent preacher on Sunday mornings, led worship, and conducted altar ministry. During the pre-transition years, I withheld my counsel during elder meetings because I knew they would be at odds with the direction the senior leader wanted to take the church. We simply were not aligned in assignment. It was not his fault, nor was it my fault.

One April night in 2012 Robin told me she thought it was time to move. By August, we were gracefully and peacefully released by the chapel leadership, and our assignment at what was to become the Journey Center began. There is a powerful difference between being differently aligned in our kingdom assignments and being rebellious, but it can be difficult to discern. Kingdom assignments can and should be diverse. It is God's plan that we all walk in our unique giftings and assignments, but we should stay in harmony one to another and under authority. Each body has a corporate vision that is supported by the many body parts.

When the overall vision of our corporate expression is vastly different than what we are called to by the Lord, there is an important decision to make. Overthrow is never the answer. It was apparent to the senior leadership at the chapel that I was being moved into a different corporate vision than that at the chapel. In unity, we agreed it was time for our family to move into our new assignment. The fruit is the evidence. Sadly, I have been in more than one senior meeting where subordinates attempted to overthrow the appointed leader. Happily, I have never seen it work, though on more than one occasion I was the elder who stopped it cold.

Leading those in authority will never come with a tone of accusation. The Holy Spirit does not speak in that tone, nor one of guilt, shame, or condemnation. The Holy Spirit always speaks in tones of redemption and restoration. When and if issues arise that need to be confronted, kingdom culture demands scriptural principles be applied.

While it is an absolute leadership mandate to train, equip, empower, and release our subordinates, it is a great blessing to be empowered and released by our subordinates. When a familiar spirit is conquered, and we recognize and embrace the mantle carried by our covering, promotion ensues. Disavowing the familiar spirit is mandatory. Familiarity has no role in the kingdom. It speaks only in accusation and disrespect. Familiarity speaks only to the past and never to the present or the future. I love Graham Cooke's phrase that "Holy Spirit prophecy speaks from our present fullness to our future completion." Familiarity speaks from our past to limit our present and prohibit our future. Gone unchecked, it is a destroyer that works up and down the leadership schematic.

The most powerful way to lead those in authority over us is to recognize their mantle and commit absolutely to empowering them. I met with Dr. Tom Jones of Global Awakening a few years back. I had watched how he and Randy Clark interacted. Randy is the founder and visionary of Global, and he and Scott Lowmaster are similar visionaries. They are always seeing new possibilities.

I asked Tom for counsel on how to work with a brilliant visionary that seems to be twenty steps ahead of "reality." Tom's response was brilliant. He said that in his ten years with Randy, while he does not hesitate to provide wise counsel, he has never told Randy, "No." Though Randy gives Tom a level of veto power, Tom recognizes that Randy's apostolic gift needs the freedom to dream and make things happen that others may not see. That is walking in and under authority. As subordinates, we can lead the people in authority over us without using hidden agendas to gain higher positions; rather, we receive great bounty from our heavenly Father and our leaders by our submissiveness to empower our leaders to walk in their God-given gifts freely.

Section 4

~

SUSTAINED GROWTH

Chapter 13

Understanding Assignment

Among the signs we are growing into our leadership mantle are when offers come pouring in. Discerning sons and daughters will recognize God's promotion at work in our lives and want to be part of it. His favor will be evidenced in many facets of our life. Everything our hands touch turns to His gold, both tangibly and intangibly. When we petition heaven, we see the physical and spiritual evidence of our authority and have complete faith we are changing atmospheric conditions in areas where we do not see evidence. We can be at peace internally with ourselves and externally with others, though it is impossible to please everyone.

As our internal atmosphere says, "Jesus," our external atmosphere speaks authority. As this occurs, we will be offered appointments in positions of leadership at an increased rate. Each time we must carefully consider who is offering the position. Is it the Lord, or is it man? Titles and positions are always offered via human conduit but not always by the direction of the

> As our internal atmosphere say, "Jesus," our external atmosphere speaks authority.

Holy Spirit. Jesus's words in Luke 10 ring in the ears of every senior leader in the kingdom: "The harvest truly is great, but the laborers are few; therefore, pray the Lord of the harvest to send out laborers into His harvest."[1]

The lack of laborers is a challenge faced by church leaders every day. The harvest is truly great, and the laborers are truly few. This conundrum is too frequently "corrected" by leadership offering positions to people who are ill-fitted to complete the task. The result can be positions filled by those ill-equipped or out of alignment with God's plan. This hard truth is one I have fallen victim to by being placed in ill-fitting assignments too many times. Over the years I have been short-handed in my various kingdom assignments. In haste, I have hired or appointed those who, after much unproductive time, learned they were either unwilling or unable to handle the assignment.

I have also accepted positions for which I was unfit, one of which cost my family and me dearly. I accepted this position based on a desire to provide for my family. What I did not do was pray and seek God's wisdom, an approach to making decisions I had not been taught or astute enough to learn. Because I had not been trained or equipped, I was not ready to be empowered or released. I was autonomous. The four years I spent in this position steadily led me to personal decline. In trying to make it work, I went deep into debt, created a tax consequence, and by the time I finally quit, I had severed my conscience in ways that took me many years to recover from emotionally. I had not yet learned to present myself before the Lord or learned that Jesus had an interest in my life at a micro-level.

This is not to say there are not times we just act. We walk by His Spirit every day, looking for opportunities to advance the kingdom. Jesus was not referring to acts of service when He said the laborers are few. He was referring to those few who willingly accept His leadership mantle.

---

1 Luke 10:2

However, concerning our kingdom assignments, a problem arises when we take matters into our own hands and take promotion prematurely or make major decisions purely out of need. Jesus recognized and was able to delineate those who were ready for promotion from those who needed more time to learn and to grow. Note that moments before He appointed seventy unnamed followers to the kingdom work, He refused appointment to others. Luke 9:57–62 recounts this:

> Now it happened as they journeyed on the road, that someone said to Him, "Lord, I will follow You wherever You go."
>
> And Jesus said to him, "Foxes have holes and birds of the air have nests, but the Son of Man has nowhere to lay His head."
>
> Then He said to another, "Follow Me."
>
> But he said, "Lord, let me first go and bury my father."
>
> Jesus said to him, "Let the dead bury their own dead, but you go and preach the kingdom of God."
>
> And another also said, "Lord, I will follow You, but let me first go and bid them farewell who are at my house."
>
> But Jesus said to him, "No one, having put his hand to the plow, and looking back, is fit for the kingdom of God."

Jesus modeled a life of prayer and seeking the Father's heart in a way many of us miss. His steady and constant need to consult the Father provided the base for His sinless life. His decision-making was flawless. He knew what men were thinking,[2] who was ready to accept assignments, and who was not. Jesus knew those referenced in the story in Luke 9 were not aware of the cost associated with the appointment

---

2 Matthew 9:4

they sought. There are many believers poised in a "First let me do this and first let me do that" place in their hearts.

Jesus appointed those who would eventually fall away, and it was not limited to Judas Iscariot. John 6:66 shows of a mass exodus of disciples away from Jesus. They could not understand; therefore, they did not abide with His words. I believe many of them returned at some point in their lives. There are some who have the maturity to receive promotion but lack the character development to remain in that position.

Responsibility of appointing others does not rest on those tasked to appoint alone. Responsibility of accepting the appointments is equally shared by those who are being offered positions. Many good-intentioned leaders prematurely offer positions with the hope of growth and maturity. The key word here is "prematurely". We are all promoted but perhaps not fully capable of the presented assignment. That is what the Holy Spirit and training and equipping are for. When accepting kingdom assignments, remaining centered in His will for our lives and not getting ahead of His plans and timing are mandated by heaven.

Many people gravitate toward desired appointments for their various perceived benefits without counting the cost.[3] In truth, titles and positions are never based on a desire for authority, affirmation, pay, status, and/or clout. God-given titles and positions are always service-oriented, and there is always a cost. Over years of growth, I have happily accepted promotions in position without carefully weighing what was being asked of me. Worse, I have accepted positions without adequately presenting the cost to my family. While always gracious, my wife, Robin, has been forced to pay a cost she did not sign up for when I circumvent the wisdom of unity in decision-making.

The process of being appointed requires input from the Holy Spirit. It is easy to accept a promotion in reaction to some great action or words

---

3 Luke 14:26–35

from others, but it is our responsibility to always look deeper into our own hearts. As we mature, we consider appointments not for what we get out of them but for what we are able to give. Assignments attained for selfish gain are always temporary and cannot be sustained without repositioning our hearts.

A self-centered play for position or title lacks character. Jesus acknowledges this dynamic in Luke 9. We should not alter our personalities with a purpose to position ourselves for promotion. Our position as sons and daughters of God is a life of developing our hearts' connection with the Father, partnered with Jesus and empowered by the Holy Spirit. Father God authors and owns our promotion. When we circumvent His timing or His mantle, we come out of alignment with His purposes in our lives.

Understanding our assignments requires absolute trust in God and His timing. Even when our calling is clear, we need to remain intentional to maintain that trust for provision and timing. God is a master chess player. He has the moves all figured out well in advance.[4] He gives us prophetic visions and dreams to clue us in to future events. I love it when God gives

> Understanding our assignments requires absolute trust in Him.

me a glimpse of His glory to come, but I never want to use that glimpse to get ahead of His timing, partially because we see only in part, and I know my understanding is incomplete. He uses visions and dreams to keep us pressing toward the goal[5] while keeping us focused on the here and now.

Waiting for God's timing is especially difficult for younger leaders who are anxious to get on with their calling. I have heard many young leaders who announce themselves prematurely as apostles, prophets, or pastors

---

4 Jeremiah 29:11

5 Philippians 3:14

because of a prophetic word someone gave them or even a word they correctly heard for themselves. They believe themselves ready for the mantle and want leadership to acknowledge a promotion they believe is rightfully theirs. Hunger for God's promotion is a good thing, yet as He knows what we are ready for and when we are ready for it, our focus should be on seeking His will and trusting His timing.

"Glory that you understand and know me"

I love that the Lord gives us permission to pursue Him so intently as to understand Him and know His ways.

> Thus says the LORD: "Let not the wise man glory in his wisdom, Let not the mighty man glory in his might, nor let the rich man glory in his riches; But let him who glories glory in this, that he understands and knows Me, That I am the LORD, exercising lovingkindness, judgment, and righteousness in the earth. For in these I delight," says the LORD.[6]

Jesus needed significant time praying alone with the Father to accomplish this. When He says "pray the Lord of the harvest send out laborers into the harvest," it is because that is what He did. We may never fully understand the level Jesus prayed for His disciples, but there are insights Jesus prayed frequently for the people the Lord would send him. Jesus did this because He was intentional about who He appointed and knew the cost.

Consider the fact that Jesus prayed all night before choosing His disciples,[7] a hodge-podge of Johnny lunchbox workers, tax collecting societal rejects, zealots, doubters, and a thief. When appointing these

---

6 Jeremiah 9:23–24

7 Luke 6:12–13

most trusted positions from this data pool, it is easy to see why Jesus prayed so much. Consequently, as a senior leader in any organization, you must realize that this step must not be skipped.

When determining the cost of accepting an offered position, we should first consider whether the offer is from God or from man outside His will. This is what set the disciples apart from others who did not follow[8] and comes before counting the cost. Every major decision should undergo this process. It is frequently not a time-consuming event for those walking by the spirit. Sons and daughters hungry to be laborers for Jesus stay on constant alert for such appointments.

When we walk by the spirit, appointments are many times the final confirmation of what we have been hearing, and we will know it instantly. We are designed to be in covenant one to another, through marriage and as believers. For any major appointments, wisdom calls for confirmation from the Holy Spirit and with the people we are partnered with.

It is wonderful that after his conversion, Paul the apostle went immediately to marketplace ministry,[9] but his mantle as apostle took ten years.[10] This ten-year training from AD 36 to AD 46 was a necessary part of preparing Paul for His calling. These were years of intense training under the watchful eyes of Barnabas and the apostles. Paul came out of those years a refined leader.[11] In understanding our assignments, we need to embrace the required season of training and equipping. This all starts with a daily pursuit of God and what He has for us each day.

---

8   Luke 9:59; Mark 10:21

9   Acts 9:20

10   Acts 13:1–3

11   Acts 20:18–38

Chapter 14

Building a Team or Staff

God's promotion is always in understanding, wisdom, and revelation, and as we are promoted these attributes are honed and sharpened through deepened relationships with the Holy Spirit.[1] When promotion is accompanied by genuine humility, our city on a hill begins to gain in elevation.[2] As the elevation of the hill upon which we are influencing climbs, we will inevitably be offered titles and positions we are predestined to obtain, some of which will afford us the privilege of building a team or staff.

For the purposes of this chapter, we will consider a team to be two or more volunteers who agree to serve under authority to assist in completing an assignment. A staff will be defined as any number of paid individuals who agree to serve under authority to assist in completing an assignment. We must consider the particular nuances of each when we form and manage the members.

---

1 John 16:7–16

2 Matthew 5:14

When building a team, it is important to shop for experience and exuberance. Over the years, I have perceived that the strongest senior leaders tend to have worked their way up the ranks. We draw on the experiences of being part of a team or staff. Many young leaders in this generation want to skip this crucial part of their development. There is a tendency for the flesh to want immediate position and title granted solely through classroom experience.

In the army my job was driving line officers in an M151A2, a standard army Jeep. I served several captains from both Officer Candidacy Schools (OCS); these are former enlisted soldiers who become officers through OCS. I also drove officers from West Point. It was apparent to us grunts that OCS officers tended to be much more realistic and less self-serving than those fresh out of West Point. OCS officers had "been there and done that," while the young West Point officers seemed more interested in their own vertical climb than the health and safety of their men. Higher education certainly plays an integral role in developing leaders, but learning without experience is incomplete training. In other words, grunts trust other grunts over those who have not yet gotten muddy and bloody.

> Learning without experience is incomplete training.

No matter the type of organization, there are immeasurable skills to be learned and honed as a team or staff. After all, we are interfacing our flaws among the flaws of others. Through working out our flaws, we learn many things. We learn dying to our flesh,[3] we learn to forgive quickly,[4] we learn the value and the sum of the parts,[5] and we learn how to serve one another,[6] just to name a few. We learn the skill of walking

---

3 Romans 8

4 Colossians 3:13

5 1 Corinthians 12:12–27

6 Ruth 1:16–17

under authority with our bodies, minds, and spirits. Each developed skill builds us up and builds on other skills.

As our obedience and service will invite a promotion that requires us to build teams, our years of getting muddy and bloody will be most helpful as we select partners in our assignments. It is tempting to build a team or staff from an A-list of people. A-listers are those with whom we are already aligned personally or professionally, or those we hold in high esteem. We can cite scripture to back up this method,[7] yet as the size of our assignments increase, we quickly find that focusing only on those with whom we are already aligned is not practical and will leave out many awesome up-and-comers. We can also fall into a system of selecting whoever is available and willing, yet we find many times those who are available are available for a reason. Holy Spirit guidance is a good thing. Also a spiritual gift test can be a great asset in helping align desire to serve with the task or assignment.

While Scripture has many examples of how God determined the makeup of His army (Gideon's 300, David's mighty men), Jesus's selection process is by far the most striking. Assisted by the Holy Spirit, Jesus selected men and women from across the cultural landscape. During His time on earth, Jesus's most senior appointees were taken from the fabric of the common and rejected. Through the rough-and-tumble personality of Peter, Jesus formed His church, and in an adulteress Samaritan He resurrected a city. Through a hated tax collector, Jesus presented the gospel of the kingdom. He gave every chance for the His betrayer, Judas, to change his destiny. After Jesus's resurrection, He chose the most highly educated and communicative Saul of Tarsus, a man who had been intent to eradicate Jesus's followers, to write nearly one-half of the New Testament.

Over the last twenty years or more I have been positioned to hire and fire, select and cut, chose and reject sons and daughters in numerous

---

7 Judges 7

capacities and positions. In coaching over one thousand games, I have been part of fifty-eight team tryouts in which young men or women worked extremely hard just to make the team or get a few minutes of playing time. As a regional manager of a large forestry firm, I hired staff. As part of an executive committee of one of New York State's premier lobby groups, I was tasked with hiring the executive director. As owner of King Timberlands Consulting Group, I select and form my staff. As executive director of iMatter, I have built a team with a dozen team leads all tasked with building teams of their own. In all, I have been tasked with, or have been part of a small group of people who are tasked with, selecting hundreds of candidates to fill various positions to accomplish various goals. It is frequently not easy.

It is important to recognize that even though some people are given an opportunity, they will not mature enough to take advantage of it. It is one thing to make a team; it is another to be able to stay on it. Jesus selected Judas knowing he was going to betray Him. At the very least, Jesus knew He was going to be betrayed, and He discerned which disciple was going to do it somewhere along the way *and* kept Him on the team.

Experienced leaders look for people others have overlooked. Each of us has experienced what it is like to be selected for a team or a position by another person who went against the popular view. This first happened to me in the army when First Sergeant Norman Bowden saw something in me that both others and I did not. He trained and equipped me, then released

> Experienced leaders look for people others have overlooked.

the soldier in me I wanted to be but had not found the way to become. Another time someone went against the grain to choose me was when my wife Robin said yes! Let the head-scratching begin. I am blessed that my wife is a "yes" person and very happy she did not overthink her answer when I asked her to be my life partner.

Like me, there are many wonderful late bloomers just waiting for the right leader to offer them a chance to make a contribution. In reality, these can be your hardest workers and most loyal allies. They are used to being overlooked and are grateful for a leader with enough foresight to see the gold they carry.

The selection process affords sons and daughters opportunities to grow and mature as part of our teams or staff. If we provide the correct training, equipping, empowering, and releasing, it will be up to them to succeed. Some will not succeed and will need to circle the mountain again. In this way we can partner with the Father of Lights in His promotion process.

As the senior leader, we have to be reconciled that not all who accept an invitation for position will be able to handle the maturity requirements, and they may need to step down or even be removed. This is not always due to a faulty promotion or even because of a lack of training. Sometimes it is simply that those who are promoted do not grow in maturity at a pace that allows them to remain in the promotion.

We have all experienced a taste of God's promotion we cannot handle. If promotion feeds our egos, we gravitate toward prideful acts and mistreating His kids. If gone uncorrected, it will result in the promotion being at least temporarily suspended.[8] God is not angry with us when He demotes us; He is patient and faithful to facilitate our maturity. He disciplines those He loves.[9]

Recruiting "Yes" People

In selecting teams, I like Jesus's model of being both the recruiter and the recruited. Jesus recruited "yes" people. "Yes" people are not blind

---

8 Genesis 37

9 Hebrews 12:6

> Mature "Yes" people have learned to rest
> while completing their assignments.

followers; rather, they simply have a can-do mind-set. They are not always looking for reasons something cannot or should not be done. They focus their energy on how an assignment can be accomplished. "Yes" people have the right attitude from the start, and their first inclination is to say, "Yes."

We do not find "yes" people with abundant time on their couch. They do not go home every night at five o'clock. "Yes" people understand rest is necessary to survive, yet mature "yes" people have learned to rest while completing their assignments. They stand out because they accomplish great things in the kingdom and do it in a way in which anxiety and stress are not oozing out of them. Instead, they walk in the peace that comes from abiding in Jesus.

"Yes" people are overachievers. They are accustomed to detractors telling them what cannot be done, so they easily press through others' limitations. Mature overachievers define success differently and define failure differently than naysayers do. To an overachiever, success is defined more by the fully explored vision than the visual outcome.[10] From each venture, overachievers learn valuable lessons, then apply what they learned to assist in fulfilling their assignments. To an overachiever, failure is neglecting their assignments or delegating their assignments to others. They recognize the 168 hours we have in a week are a precious commodity and reject the notion they can be wasted with no effect. I find the attrition rate of "yes" people is far less, and the promotion rate is far greater, than those whose first instinct is no.

---

10   2 Corinthians 4:18

Being Recruited

Jesus was adept at being recruited. He lived famously by the words He said and the deeds He did.[11] He perfectly balanced intimate life with the Father, close friendships, and life among the people. When others sought Jesus, He never turned them away. He set the standards and offered positions. His approach was always brilliant and is illustrated in Luke 8:26–39:

> Then they sailed to the country of the Gadarenes, which is opposite Galilee. And when He stepped out on the land, there met Him a certain man from the city who had demons for a long time. And he wore no clothes, nor did he live in a house but in the tombs. When he saw Jesus, he cried out, fell down before Him, and with a loud voice said, "What have I to do with You, Jesus, Son of the Most High God? I beg You, do not torment me!" For He had commanded the unclean spirit to come out of the man. For it had often seized him, and he was kept under guard, bound with chains and shackles; and he broke the bonds and was driven by the demon into the wilderness. Jesus asked him, saying, "What is your name?" And he said, "Legion," because many demons had entered him. And they begged Him that He would not command them to go out into the abyss.
>
> Now a herd of many swine was feeding there on the mountain. So they begged Him that He would permit them to enter them. And He permitted them. Then the demons went out of the man and entered the swine, and the herd ran violently down the steep place into the lake and drowned.

---

11 John 14:11–12

> When those who fed them saw what had happened, they
> fled and told it in the city and in the country. Then they
> went out to see what had happened, and came to Jesus,
> and found the man from whom the demons had departed,
> sitting at the feet of Jesus, clothed and in his right mind.
> And they were afraid. They also who had seen it told them
> by what means he who had been demon-possessed was
> healed. Then the whole multitude of the surrounding
> region of the Gadarenes asked Him to depart from them,
> for they were seized with great fear. And He got into the
> boat and returned.
>
> Now the man from whom the demons had departed
> begged Him that he might be with Him. But Jesus sent
> him away, saying, "Return to your own house, and tell
> what great things God has done for you." And he went
> his way and proclaimed throughout the whole city what
> great things Jesus had done for him.

This beautiful story should be replayed many times in a leader's life.
Suffering sons and daughters recruit us for deliverance and assurance.
We are positioned to partner with the Holy Spirit to position them
appropriately in their assignments. It is wonderful that though the
delivered man wanted to join Jesus's traveling staff, Jesus had another
assignment in mind. Also, it is perfect this once demon-possessed man
turned the city who had rejected Jesus by the word of his testimony.
Luke 8:40 says, "So it was, when Jesus returned, that the multitude
welcomed Him, for they were all waiting for Him."

Jesus walked with Holy Spirit wisdom in the decisions as to whom to
place on His immediate staff and whom He would send out to other
assignments. He always considered the individual while keeping His
mission on track. All were connected, and no one was rejected. When
assembling and maintaining teams, Jesus is the example.

Chapter 15

Study to Show Thyself Approved

Recently Robert Henderson of Global Reformers spoke at the Journey Center. Robert has a marvelous understanding of the courts system of heaven. During his presentation he saw a demonic spirit of dullness active in our region.

I never really considered how a "spirit of dullness" could come over a group of people, so I studied the Scriptures and found no shortage of scripture on the topic. Jesus addressed the topic frequently:

> MATTHEW 13:13–15: Therefore I speak to them in parables, because seeing they do not see, and hearing they do not hear, nor do they understand. And in them the prophecy of Isaiah is fulfilled, which says:
>
> > "Hearing you will hear and shall not understand,
> > And seeing you will see and not perceive;
> > For the hearts of this people have grown dull.
> > Their ears are hard of hearing,
> > And their eyes they have closed,
> > Lest they should see with their eyes and hear with

their ears,
Lest they should understand with their hearts and turn,
So that I should heal them."

MATTHEW 15:16: So Jesus said, "Are you also still without understanding?"

MATTHEW 16:11: How is it you do not understand that I did not speak to you concerned bread?—but to beware of the leaven of the Pharisees and Sadducees.

LUKE 24:25: Then He said to them, "O foolish ones, and slow of heart to believe in all the prophets have spoken."

JOHN 8:43: Why do you not understand My speech? Because you are not able to listen to My word.

JOHN 14:9: Jesus said to him, "Have I been with you so long, and yet you have not known Me, Philip? He who as seen Me has seen the Father; so how can you say, 'Show us the Father'?"

Dullness is a direct result of the lack of study that reflects a spiritual laziness. Spiritual laziness promotes a poverty approach to understanding and knowledge, whereas hunger is an intense quest for truth. Truth is an inconvenience to our flesh, as dullness is incongruent with our spirit man. In essence, dullness is trading truth for a lie[1] and places great limitations on our growth and maturity. Dullness leaves us relying on our own instincts and intuition instead of Holy Spirit-led discernment.

---

1 Romans 1:25

Where discernment is from the Holy Spirit, confirmed by knowing the heart of God learned through abiding and study, intuition is our self-generated instincts learned from observational science.

We marvel at how well Jesus knew Scripture and the Father. By twelve years of age He was fully engaged in a lifestyle of study that proved His knowledge of Scripture and the Father's heart[2] after His ministry began. Jesus challenges us in the same way He challenged himself.[3] When reading the gospels, it does not take much imagination to feel as though we are standing right there while He is teaching.

It is easy to love Jesus's direct nature when we pursue truth. We will embrace straight talk from someone who loves so unconditionally, whose only motivation is for our very best. Jesus frequently called out the disciples' spiritual laziness as He did their lack of faith.[4] He challenges us when we use our fleshly intuition. While the disciples had Jesus in the flesh, they did not have the Holy Spirit in the same capacity as Jesus did and we do. That did not come until after Jesus was resurrected. The disciples were relegated to take Jesus at His word and deeds;[5] we get His word, deeds, *and* the Holy Spirit, yet Jesus still directly challenged their dullness.

Spiritual dullness is not to be tolerated by the mature believer. Ours is an intense relationship with the Godhead, a continuing educational process of discovering and uncovering mysteries and truth for the glory of Him who resides in us for our benefit and those we impact with that glory, a glory that was given to the Son by the Father and then transferred to us from the Son.[6] Our ongoing education is driven by a hunger for more. We do not pray for God to give us more—He has

---

2 John 5:19

3 John 15:7

4 John 14:9

5 John 14:11

6 John 17:22

given us everything. We pray that we learn how to access more and boldly seek out all He has for us.

Study to Show Thyself Approved

Each time we are promoted in the kingdom, we are afforded the privilege of a return to kindergarten in many ways. God is always faithful to do His part in grace and mercy, but we need to do ours. Too often promotion offers an open door to a prideful heart that says, "I can handle this," but the truth is that you cannot, and neither can I. The cool thing is—neither could Jesus. John 5:19 tells us, "Then Jesus answered and said to them 'Most assuredly, I say to you the Son can do nothing of Himself, but what He sees the Father do; for whatever He does the Son also does in like manner.'" Then, in John 8:28–29, we read, "Then Jesus said to them, 'When you lift up the Son of Man, then you will know that I am He, and that I do nothing of Myself; but as My Father taught Me. I speak those things. And He who sent Me is with Me. The father has not left Me alone, for I always do those things that please Him.'" Did you ever wonder how the Father taught Jesus? Was it through some form of impartation available only to Jesus? Was it a mandatory training program the Father forced on the Son given His status as Son of the Most High and the nature of the assignment? Did Jesus have the option to say no? At what age did this training start? Certainly it started long before the age of twelve, when Jesus's "understanding and answers" amazed the teachers in the temple.

We can be so driven by other desires, tasks, work, hobbies, or down time that studying God's Word and heart can take a back seat or have no place in our lives at all. If gone uncorrected, this becomes a major issue for us as leaders as we are promoted, ultimately becoming a ceiling for our promotion. I have known many pastors, including myself, who have fallen into a life of studying only for the purpose of preaching and teaching, which comes at the expense of personal growth. The purpose of studying is to learn about the Godhead, and preaching and teaching flows from that knowledge.

Paul instructs Timothy, "Be diligent [study] to present yourself approved to God, a worker who does not need to be ashamed, rightly dividing the word of truth."[7] Paul goes on to say,

> But you must continue in the things which you have learned and been assured of, knowing from whom you had learned them, and that from childhood you have known the Holy Scriptures, which are able to make you wise for salvation through faith which is in Christ Jesus. All scripture is given by inspiration of God and is profitable for doctrine, for reproof, for correction, for instruction in righteousness, that the man of God may be complete, thoroughly equipped for every good work.[8]

Study is not self-serving but spirit-serving. There is a depth of John 15:7 that goes well beyond being granted anything we desire. Jesus said, "If you abide in me and my word abides in you, you will ask what you desire and it shall be done for you." We can safely assume Jesus was not talking about desire for pizza or a new car. The key word here is *abiding*. Abiding is not a temporary vacation spot but a full-time residency. Abiding in Him is taking up residency in the throne room of heaven. Abiding in the Word is a life dedication of study.

As we mature, the more rounded we become in word and deed. We understand becoming "all things to all people."[9] As we are conformed more and more to the likeness of Jesus Christ,[10] we are called to relate and

---

7   2 Timothy 2:15

8   John 15:7

9   1 Corinthians 9:22

10   Romans 8:29

minister throughout the ages and positions of His sons and daughters. Jesus sourced His knowledge of the heart of the Father, emboldening Him to complete His assignment and love as His Father loved.

Today we have limitless resources available—from professional institutions and universities, to Spirit-led books, devotionals, and blogs, to teaching DVDs and CDs. Each of these is important, and we should take maximum advantage of the modern era. I love our school of supernatural ministry at the Journey Center and reading books by men and woman who have learned to access a part of God I have not yet learned. These study guides create a knowledge base that drives us to the Jesus model: our abiding in Him and His word abiding in us.

Studying Opens the Possibilities

During a personal pilgrimage to Israel in 2010, I spent twenty-one days alone, during which, I have jokingly stated, I went expecting to join the "Jesus, Elijah, Moses club." I believed the experience would be so intense that I would actually feel as if I were "one the guys" in the transfiguration scene. In truth, it never occurred to me that it might actually be possible. Now, years later, because of a life of abiding in Jesus and His word, the joke is becoming a possibility. If allowed, the Holy Spirit removes any limitations we place on His depth. My limitations were tied to the limitations I put on a limitless God. Books and schools help facilitate the introduction of a life of abiding in Him and the Word, and if Jesus truly has much more He wants to tell us when we are ready,[11] our job is to get ready.

I do not like making a religion out of reading the Word but prefer a life of abiding in it. The Holy Spirit will lead us in this. Jesus sanctifies and washes us with water by the Word.[12] As we spend time

---

11 John 16:12

12 Ephesians 5:26

being washed by the Word, God's glory is revealed in a way others' words cannot reveal. The truth of the Word frees us from our chains. Because Jesus is truth, studying Him is the pathway to truth. "Then Jesus said to those Jews who believed Him, 'If you abide in My word, you are My disciples indeed. And you shall know the truth, and the truth shall make you free.'"[13]

---

13 John 8:31–32

Chapter 16

Celebrate!

O ur heavenly Father is an unapologetic celebrator who resides in the celebration capital of time and before time. He is predisposed to enjoy all His creation and all His co-laborers. His atmosphere is one of rejoicing. Celebration is a required outcome of understanding. He celebrates because He is celebration. Our God fully comprehends who He is and who we are. He has perfectly set us up to receive His glory and rejoices in the process. Though pain is the offshoot of sin, He knows its temporary status. He has put pain's limits in place and subjected it to His timing.[1]

God initiated mankind in celebration of His glory. He celebrated for the entire six days He was creating the heavens and the earth— He celebrated every creation and every act.

> God initiated mankind in celebration of His glory.

When He created male and female, He blessed them and celebrated His handiwork in them. After sin entered the garden of Eden, God, through endless love, adjusted His approach to maintain a relationship with His children. Restitution and redemption were purposed for

---

1 Mark 13:32

restoration. The required restitution of the Old Testament was paid in full with Jesus's redemptive death on the cross, which resulted in our full restoration. That is worth celebrating.

God knows there are no little victories. He is fully bought into our success in every new discovery of His perfection, and with each step we make toward Him, He celebrates. The Old Testament boasts of God's celebratory heart. From the Creation in Genesis to the celebration feasts during the Exodus and to each corresponding turn from sin in Judges, from Solomon's building of the temple to Nehemiah's rebuilding of the wall, Father God celebrated our Bible heroes' obedience.

Jesus emulated His Father.[2] He compared the kingdom of heaven to a wedding feast,[3] and it is indeed so. He advises us to a level of rejoicing in heaven that perfectly shouts of the Father's celebrative style, noted in Luke 15:10: "Likewise, I say to you, there is joy in the presence of the angels of God over one sinner who repents." In Luke 15:22-24 Jesus told parables of the Father's fondness of celebrating: "But the father said to his slaves, 'Quickly bring out the best robe and put it on him, and put a ring on his hand and sandals on his feet; and bring the fattened calf, kill it, and let us eat and celebrate; for this son of mine was dead and has come to life again; he was lost and has been found.' And they began to celebrate."

When we do not take the appropriate and intentional amount of time to celebrate God's handiwork in and through others, we become at odds with the Father's heart of rejoicing. This is the precise position of the prodigal son's older brother. He was so internally focused on his own position that he would not rejoice at the return of his brother.

Jonah had the same problem. In Jonah 4 we see how he refused to celebrate with the Father. When the people of Nineveh obeyed the

---

2 John 5:19–20

3 Matthew 22:2

word of the Lord and turned, the Father celebrated them by relenting from pending disaster. Jonah, refusing to celebrate, left the city and sat pouting underneath a juniper tree. He gave way to an ungrateful heart to the extent that the only thing he could find joy in was a plant that provided him shade. He could not celebrate the life of others, only what gave him pleasure.

It is a sign of significant maturity when we celebrate promotion in others as much as we celebrate our own. A good heart position check is to gauge our response when the people we consider under our authority are promoted to equal status. If we have a hard time celebrating others' promotion, we have a need to mature in the area of envy and jealousy. If we find our first inclination is to rejoice in the promotion of others, we walk in a level of maturity with that of our savior.

Jesus exemplifies this in John 17:22: "And the glory which You gave Me I have given them, that they may be one just as We are one." Jesus not only celebrated the reunion of us with the Father, but He actively endorses the Father to us of His same position. Jesus knew while the Father is the Author and Owner of our promotion, His partnership was integral to our attaining all the Father intended. Celebrating the promotion of others is a wonderful opportunity to celebrate and demonstrate that we understand Who is the Author of promotion.

God does not seem too worried that all this celebration over us will give us a fat head. In fact, I am not sure he is worried about our pride at all. He knows how to handle pride when it shows up. We have all experienced our own version of being in Joseph's pit or inside Jonah's whale, and we have the tragic examples of King Saul and Nebuchadnezzar that the Holy Spirit can remind us of.

I am convinced I under-celebrate. As a coach, I was so focused on each team playing as well as they were capable of that I would forget players liked to celebrate wins, scores, successes, seasons, and teams. I have inappropriately put my teams in a state of "We can't do anything right" with the predictable result of a reduced effort for excellence. If left uncorrected, team morale would plummet as coaches became known more as dictators with a whistle, constantly reminding them of their lack instead of being known as great coaches who partner with players to attain the goal of being the best they can be. For me, I preferred being known as a loving father figure who firmly, and sometimes loudly but gently, leads teams to success.

My lack of celebrating little victories was due largely to my doubt of our successful outcome. In order to put ourselves in positions to win championships, we need to address areas of weakness and grow as a team. However, over the years I learned that this is a short-sighted vision. These young men learned more about life throughout the season than from a single game, even if that game won the championship banner.

Ours is never a job focused only on the faults or lack of others. When leaders over-focus on what is wrong, an internal sense develops within the staff or team that nothing is good enough. No matter what their efforts, how high the attained results, how excellent they become, the only message that permeates from "perfection drivers" is that teams or staff must work much harder to do better. That in itself is the proverbial carrot dangling on the end of a stick in front of the cart. It is not possible to get the carrot, because it is incongruent with God's heart. In the kingdom of God, Satan has already been checkmated. The game is already won. The time to celebrate is now.

> The game is already won. The time to celebrate is now.

Leaders should be intentional to build celebratory habits both internally and with our teams and staff. It starts with celebrating the Godhead. The best understanding we have about the person of the Father still puts tremendous limits on who He actually is because the God of the universe has no end. His depth cannot be fathomed nor His love fully comprehended. That is something worth celebrating.

If we are quiet, we can hear
Him celebrating us.

God chose to form us from His image and gave us a place in His life; Jesus ransomed our sin and transferred His place to us; the glory the Father gave the son is the same glory the Son gave us. These are worth celebrating.

The Father surrounds us with brothers and sisters, fellow bond-servants, co-heirs with Jesus, His only begotten Son. That is something to celebrate.

We rejoice with the angels over each sinner who repents. We celebrate the birth of each son and daughter and each baptism. These are things to celebrate.

If we are quiet, we can hear God celebrating us. Sometimes He even gets loud. At 9:30 PM on the evening of September 29, 2013, my wife was on a cruise with her mother, and I was home alone. It was a Saturday night, and I was postured before the Lord, listening and waiting on Him. In this quiet place I whispered to Him, "Father, will you help me steward my time?" This was spoken from a humble heart desired to please Him and show Him how grateful I was for all He had given me. As soon as I spoke, His presence filled the room with the kind of tangible presence that leaves us frozen as a statue, unable to breathe or move.

The Father said, "Son, I will indeed help you steward your time. Because you have been faithful [here He showed me specific glimpses of my faithfulness], I will intervene, and this will be the outcome." He then gave me glimpses of the glory that would take place as He helped me steward my time.

Then for the next two and half hours I was flat on my back basking in His love for me. I could feel the heat of His breath. I have never experienced anything like it. At 12:30 AM I was so overcome with the act of celebration that He was engaged in over me that I cried out in a loud, broken voice, "How can you do this? How can you make me feel like I'm your most special son?"

He responded with the kindest, most loving voice I had ever heard. He said, "You are my unique design. I made you, and I made you so special to me. I can celebrate you if I want to."

I believe we are much more at risk with undervaluing ourselves and others than overvaluing. God said, "Let Us make man in Our image, according to Our likeness"[4] and then went to work, and He does not clone. In the history of the world, there are no two people on earth who have been designed exactly the same way with precisely the same mixture of attributes of the Godhead. He is so encompassing that it takes every son and daughter from the beginning of time to the end of time to adequately represent who He is.

Mature, godly leaders walk by the Spirit of God. Through seeking wisdom and abiding in Jesus and His Word, strong leaders walk in an awareness of their promotion and partner with the Godhead in the promotion of others. We carry the jurisdictional authority transferred to us by Jesus to change the atmosphere from lack of hope to one of hope in Jesus. We celebrate the Godhead, and the Godhead celebrates us.

If He celebrates with us, it is because He understands who we are, and we in turn should celebrate with others over every victory we encounter together, because God has authored and owns our promotion. This is very much worth celebrating.

---

4 Genesis 1:26

Made in the USA
Lexington, KY
28 February 2017